Entrepreneurial Marketing

How do you sell an innovative product to a market that does not yet exist? Entrepreneurial businesses often create products and services based on radically new technology that have the power to change the marketplace. Existing market research data will be largely irrelevant in these cases, making sales and marketing of innovative new products especially challenging to entrepreneurs.

Entrepreneurial Marketing focuses on this challenge. Classic core marketing concepts, such as segmentation, positioning and the marketing mix undergo an 'extreme makeover' in the context of innovative products hitting the market. Edwin J. Nijssen stresses principles of affordable loss, experimentation and adjustment for emerging opportunities, as well as cooperation with first customers.

Containing many marketing examples of successful and cutting edge innovations (including links to websites and videos on the Internet), useful lists of key issues and instructions on how to make a one-page marketing plan, *Entrepreneurial Marketing: An Effectual Approach* provides a vital guide to successfully developing customer demand and a market for innovative new products.

This second edition has been thoroughly expanded with:

- a one-page marketing plan which now focuses on the three entrepreneurial challenges that can be easily adapted;
- coverage of the customer development process; and
- updated references and new examples.

This book provides students and entrepreneurs with the fundamental tools to succeed in marketing.

Edwin J. Nijssen is Professor of Marketing at the Eindhoven University of Technology, the Netherlands.

Given the pace of change and variety in the market today, everyone is in the entrepreneurship business, whether they realize it or not. The problem is that much of what we know from marketing big brands to static consumer groups does not translate to creating new products, services, firms and markets. As applicable to managers in large firms as it is to start-up owners, this book offers practical, rigorous and accessible insights for anyone working to create valuable novelty and make a successful market of it.

Stuart Read, *Professor, Atkinson Graduate School of Management, Willamette University, USA*

The book tackles an interesting and overlooked phenomenon, providing a useful bridge between marketing and entrepreneurship that are often treated as separated entities. It is easy to read and contains several examples, which make it a good companion for both students and practitioners. In particular, I really like its use of boxes and the 'doing-it-right' sections: they are really helpful.

Andrea Ordanini, *Professor of Marketing and Department Chair, Bocconi University, Milan, Italy*

We are currently witnessing a strong increase in entrepreneurial activity. Many of these new ventures however fail because of a lack of attention to the marketing aspect. New products need new marketing approaches that cannot be found in traditional marketing books. This book is a must read for all students of entrepreneurship as well as for all entrepreneurs who are striving for more success in the marketplace.

Geert Duysters, *Professor, Tilburg University, the Netherlands*

Ed Nijssen excels at offering entrepreneurs of radical new ideas a unique window on their market opportunity. His book provides a complete makeover of traditional marketing and effectively and seamlessly integrates the customer and new development processes.

Georges Romme, *Professor, Eindhoven University of Technology, the Netherlands*

Prof. Nijssen presents a comprehensive marketing guidebook aimed at the entrepreneur. This book will help entrepreneurs avoid big and costly marketing mistakes, by ensuring that the start-up is offering unique value to its target customer and has a competitive position it can maintain. Prof. Nijssen presents the marketing skills used by big companies and shows how they can be adapted to the needs and budget of the entrepreneur.

Anthony Di Benedetto, *Professor of Marketing and Supply Chain Management, Fox School of Business, Temple University, USA*

Entrepreneurial Marketing

An Effectual Approach
Second Edition

Edwin J. Nijssen

Routledge
Taylor & Francis Group

LONDON AND NEW YORK

Second edition published 2017
by Routledge
2 Park Square, Milton Park, Abingdon, Oxon OX14 4RN

and by Routledge
711 Third Avenue, New York, NY 10017

Routledge is an imprint of the Taylor & Francis Group, an informa business

© 2017 Edwin J. Nijssen

The right of Edwin J. Nijssen to be identified as author of this work has been asserted by him in accordance with sections 77 and 78 of the Copyright, Designs and Patents Act 1988.

First edition published by Routledge 2014

British Library Cataloguing in Publication Data
A catalogue record for this book is available from the British Library

Library of Congress Cataloging in Publication Data
A catalog record for this book has been requested

ISBN: 978-1-138-71290-4 (hbk)
ISBN: 978-1-138-71291-1 (pbk)
ISBN: 978-1-315-19986-3 (ebk)

Typeset in Times New Roman
by Sunrise Setting Ltd., Brixham, UK

Visit the companion website: www.routledge.com/cw/nijssen

Contents

Figures

Tables

Preface

Entrepreneurs often are unfamiliar with concepts of target market, price/ quality relationships, price thresholds, distributor margins and sales promotion techniques, and the importance of these factors in creating awareness and demand. Their lack of adequate knowledge in these areas results in a simplistic view of marketing problems. Many believe, for instance, that the only condition necessary for a sale is an innovative product or service. But the problem is, of course, that most new products are far from excellent, to say the least. Moreover, even excellent products will benefit from getting the price right, creating customer awareness and ensuring availability.

However, for radically new products, the challenge is even greater. Never having been seen before, these products require customers to change their cognitions and behaviours. This explains why classical or traditional marketing does not apply, and why a so-called 'effectual' approach is required. This approach starts with the technology and the new product, and uses experimentation to find the right market segment and make inroads in the market. This book explains the effectual approach and demonstrates how to use it in a creative way for marketing innovative new products.

The content of this book is the result of working with entrepreneurs and teaching graduate courses in Marketing and Innovation as well as Entrepreneurial Marketing at the Eindhoven University of Technology. The ideas have evolved over time and reflect emerging insights from entrepreneurship, new product development and marketing literature. These ideas have been identified and integrated to create a coherent method. In contrast to classical marketing, the effectual approach adopted begins with the product and looks for market segments that fit, optimising options during the process.

The method promoted complements new product development by combining it with a customer development process. Although regular new product development models include some kind of attention to the link between the new product and (latent) customer needs, customer testing and launch, typically the technical issues dominate the model and receive most resources. To compensate for this, we suggest organising the customer development process separately, as a complementary activity. This achieves a better balance and higher level of success for the entrepreneurial firm and its new product or service.

In this second edition, the text has been edited, references updated and some new examples added. The most important changes, however, pertain to chapters 7 (the one-page marketing plan and marketing mix) and 8 (the role of sales). These have been better integrated with the concept of the customer development process. This has been accomplished by suggesting that entrepreneurs focus in their one-page marketing plan on three challenges: customer value creation, building market presence and developing customer relationships. The marketing mix has been linked to the first two and the sales activities to the last challenge.

This book and new edition would not exist without the help of many people, some of whom I would like to thank in particular. First, my colleague Joost Wouters assisted me for many years in teaching the above-mentioned courses. Joost provided important feedback and examples for this book. Second, I want to thank Ties van Bommel. He offered a valuable view on issues affecting the investment and marketing decisions for new products, also often arranging guest lecturers for my courses. My wife, Martha Chorney, improved the structure, the content and the original text, making it more appealing. She also helped manage the revision. Finally, thanks are due to the anonymous reviewers whose feedback provided ideas for developing this second edition.

I hope this book offers the reader some new and exciting ideas and helps entrepreneurs to find their pot of gold.

Ed Nijssen

Chapter 1

Using marketing to create a new business with radically new ideas

Key issues

- Compare radical innovations to incremental innovations and discuss the need for changes in customer behaviour.
- Discuss the firm and customer side of a business model and explain that both need to be aligned.
- Define marketing and sales and explain the effectual marketing approach.

1.1 Entrepreneurship and radically new ideas: the need for effectuation

Every day, people come up with new ideas. Sometimes these are small ideas, but every now and then, an idea concerns something extremely innovative that can be developed into a radically new product or service: a new product that has never been seen before, but that is exciting and may even create a new product category or market. Such a new product may become a financial success for the entrepreneur who came up with the idea and decided to develop it into a business.

Entrepreneurs are people who decide to develop and market a new product or service. They feel the need, or even the urge, to pursue their luck and build their own businesses. Many entrepreneurs aim to improve existing products, rather than develop something completely new. The new hairdresser and baker around the corner could be entrepreneurs, for instance, or your neighbours who plan to start their own IT company after having worked several years for a top software firm.

The entrepreneurs in these examples compete in existing markets. Their markets involve familiar products and are clearly delineated. Consequently, these new entrepreneurs know who their customers and competitors are (such as women's hairdressers, pastry shops and customer relationship management software specialists). In these cases, they apply traditional marketing, which focuses on identifying and targeting a particular customer segment and positioning a product to address this segment's stated (or latent) needs. Its systematic and goal-oriented approach can help the nascent entrepreneur specify the value offer, develop a pricing strategy and create the right message and adequate promotional support.

In contrast, people with radically new ideas based on new technology are better defined as *high-tech* entrepreneurs. Based on new technology, their business often involves redefining existing markets by altering product categories. These entrepreneurs generally are engineers or technology enthusiasts who have developed something unique that no one has seen before or that people have only dreamed about. They see the potential of their idea and confidently go about making a business out of it, even when first customers' reactions are sceptical.

Lack of experience or business knowledge does not scare these entrepreneurial minds away. They seek financial support from venture capitalists to help finance their new business. But they usually have to invest heavily themselves, and take major personal risks too, in order to make it all come true.

Based on the *level of 'newness' of a technology*, three types of new products are generally distinguished: (1) new versions of existing products (i.e. me-too or line extensions); (2) incremental innovations; and (3) radical innovations.[1] The first category contains modestly new products: the products that have been around for some time but, with a different marketing approach, can be revived and enjoy sales growth (e.g. biologically or organically grown tomatoes). The second category of products are moderately new. They are serious extensions of existing products. These new products are similar to what we know, but there is something added, or changed, which increases value to customers. These products fit current knowledge and market structures but bring something new to the equation (e.g. LED displays or electric toothbrushes). Finally, there are radical innovations. These draw on new technology to produce products people have not seen before. These new products can often change markets, alter existing market categories or even make them obsolete (e.g. the light bulb and telephone). The more radical a product idea, the more likely people will need to change their perceptions and behaviours, but they will also need to update their definition of product categories.

For instance, whereas reduction in size of television cameras at first only resulted in extra flexibility in camera-work in large TV studio productions, subsequent miniaturisations and improvements increased the share of low-cost outdoor productions compared with studio productions. The smaller cameras' flexibility meant that it was possible for the interviewer or documentary maker to handle the camera himself or herself. This has resulted in a different perception of the function of a camera and an expanded role of the filmmaker.

In a similar way, the introduction of robots and instant diagnostics in the operating theatre has greatly improved the precision and success in tumour removal. This new and useful technology has brought about substantial changes in the profession. Surgeons see their role diminished and have to work with new medical staff who understand and manage this new, essential, medical technology.

As the previous examples suggest, marketing for radically new products differs from marketing for line extensions and incremental innovations. Because radical new products affect existing product categorisations, existing market data often do not apply, so that the business plans that are developed based on existing market data have less certainty. For example, smartphones, such as the BlackBerry and iPhone, bridged the markets of microcomputers and telephones while integrating camera functions. Obviously, the market size for smartphones could not be computed by simply combining or adding up the market data of computers, phones and cameras. A new product category was born that extended the existing categories. Whether such a new category emerges is not just determined by the provider but is in fact a negotiation process between early providers and their innovative customers.

Such changes in product categories are why marketing for radically new products is far from straightforward. It requires a novel marketing approach that embraces the uncertainty caused by the new technology, and realises that the market and latent needs are unpredictable. It involves well-thought-out trial-and-error or market experimentation, which consists of probing potential markets, learning from these, and probing again.[2] This approach is labelled '*effectuation*' and aims to 'transform the unexpected into opportunities'.[3] It emphasises creative thinking about the new technology and searching for the opportunities for its specific product application. Effectuation relies on the principle of 'affordable loss', meaning that marketing and other expenditures are limited, enabling the entrepreneur to make mistakes and change his or her course if necessary. The starting point is, however, not so much the market but the new technology or application and the resources the entrepreneur has or can gather via his or her network. The challenge is to help the customer understand the new product and use experimentation to optimise the product.[4] Effectual marketing is, most of all, a learning approach and process of discovery. It also is closely related to design thinking. Based on an understanding of customers' needs and technological alternatives, designers typically suggest a solution and optimise it in close interaction with users, using a process with multiple iterations.

1.2 Developing your business model

Although a good product (or service) idea is important, a new firm's (i.e. start-up's) viability and survival depends on its *business model*. A start-up's business model explains how the new firm will make money.[5] It explains why and how a new product and market opportunity become a business opportunity. It answers a set of very fundamental questions, including: What is our product (service)? Who are our prospective customers? Why and how much will these customers be willing to pay for our product (service)? How will we distribute the product? And how well will we be able to defend our business from competitor attack?

A business model works if three requirements are met: (1) the start-up's new product has positive customer value; (2) a certain group of customers is convinced that the new product outperforms alternatives in the marketplace; and (3) this group is willing to engage in exchange at a price that compares favourably to the development, production and distribution cost involved.

Customer value is the difference between the benefits a product delivers and the price a customer has to pay for adopting it (customer value = benefits − price). If this value is positive, its chances of being adopted increase. If the resulting value also compares favourably to the value offered by existing alternatives in the market, things look bright. However, switching costs should also be taken into consideration, for example, the time and mental effort required of customers to learn how to use the new product. Entrepreneurs often overlook these economic and psychological costs when thinking about pricing their products and predicting the speed of market penetration of their new product.

Additional requirements for a healthy business model are the size of customer base and sustainability of the start-up's positioning in the market. The number of customers attracted to the radically new product should be large enough to sustain the new firm. Further, the start-up should be able to withstand competitor attack. It should be able to develop but also defend its business. This requires a significant and sustainable competitive advantage based on a fundamental asset or capability, for instance, a patent or a unique skill (e.g. product leadership or extremely valuable customer knowledge and relationships). If the start-up has some unique competence or technology that it builds on, competitors cannot simply copy its success.

Figure 1.1 shows the business model concept. On the left-hand side, we see the value creation and delivery system of the start-up. On the right-hand side, we see the customer's consumption system. It involves prospective customers recognising the value put forward by the start-up and their willingness to pay for this value. If these two parts are 'in balance', they will stimulate continuous production and consumption. A third process highlighted is the value exchange at the bottom of the figure. It includes the negotiation between the entrepreneur and prospective customers and actual exchange. The role of marketing and sales is to align these two core processes and facilitate the third process of exchange in both the short and long run.

Different business models can be developed for similar situations or new products. Understanding the pros and cons of each model before making a choice is useful. Several categories of business models can be distinguished. First, there are the integrated business models, where a firm designs, develops, manufactures and sells its goods or services. Many firms rely on this model (e.g. traditional bakeries). Another model has firms focus on a particular role, for instance, brand and customer relationship management. Today, many firms own and sell a brand but

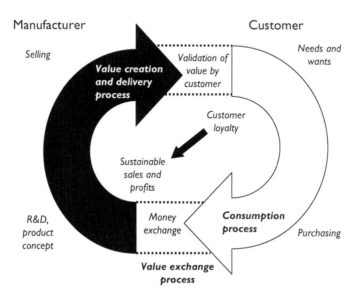

Figure 1.1 The business model concept

outsource most of the other activities. Many fashion designers and clothing companies, for example, develop and market the new products for their brand but rely on Asian partners to manufacture and ship them. Third is the so-called razor blade model, where substantial amounts of income are earned on a particular derivative facet of a product system. The name refers to the success of Gillette, the razor company. It is based on the idea of giving the handle away and earning money selling the blades. Firms applying this include telephone companies that offer a new telephone for free (or at a very low price) and make money selling calling minutes, copier firms that sell printers at a very low price and make money on cartridges, and professional document flow specialists that live from servicing their machines rather than from the margin on the machines themselves.

Doing it right – Check your business model

A useful test for any business model involves a combination of a narrative and numbers test:[6]

1   *Narrative test.* This tests asks: 'Does the story make sense?' and 'Does the proposed product or service indeed represent unique value to a group of prospective customers, and will this group be interested?' It should also address the questions of: 'Why is the start-up in a unique position to develop this value and how well is it able to protect its position?' 'Why will intermediaries also cooperate?' When the story is told, it should make sense; using this critical reflection and basic questions, the story's validity can be assessed.

2   *Numbers test.* 'Do the profit and loss add up?' 'What kind of resources are necessary, and how does this affect cost?' 'Is the anticipated stream of revenue and cash flow a sufficiently healthy basis for sustainability?' By checking assumptions of production cost and perceived customer benefits with experts one can simply see whether the numbers add up.

In each episode of the BBC television programme *Dragons' Den*, you can see how venture capitalists evaluate and scrutinise the pitch of entrepreneurs (narrative test) and ask for the general numbers of market size, cost and sales to check whether these numbers add up for the proposed start-up.[7]

The Internet, with its instant communications and interactivity, has introduced completely new business models. For instance, many firms in the game industry started by first posting games for free and then making users pay for updates. eBay gets its income from advertising rather than from selling auction space. Dutch music broker Sell-a-Band used the Internet to bring together new music artists and small investors. Small investors could listen to songs posted and buy a share in a song that then was professionally recorded and released when investor interest was sufficient. Unfortunately, the start-up did not survive. Another excellent example is the T-shirt company Threadless, which offered customers the possibility to design their own T-shirt and enter a competition to have it produced (see insert).

The Internet has boosted the opportunities for entrepreneurs. It offers a broad audience, allowing high-tech start-ups to broadcast their message 24/7 and at very low cost. Furthermore, online selling offers entrepreneurs a worldwide channel of distribution. We will look more closely at the Internet's role in the marketing of entrepreneurial firms and the marketing instruments entrepreneurs have at their disposal in Chapter 7.

Example – The Internet and new business models

Threadless is a Chicago, Illinois-based company that sells T-shirts. The firm has been making millions from 'crowd sourcing' before anyone knew what the term meant. The firm excels in social media and web marketing and it has more than 1.5 million followers on Twitter and more than 133,000 fans on Facebook. Their T-shirts typically cost $18. Founded in 2000, the start-up had immediate and huge success. In a 2008 *Newsweek* article, revenue was estimated at $30 million (for 2007). The organisation has an interesting business concept. What sets this firm apart? T-shirt designs are submitted by visitors to the website, voted on by the user and designer communities, and the top-ranked designs are produced, then sold online (Image 1.1).

The unique feature of Threadless's business model is the customer involvement. Customers are co-creators, and, as a result, they feel very empowered and extra satisfied. Co-creating and voting on the designs increases the positivity of their attitude towards the company and its T-shirts. It also increases customers' willingness to buy the shirts, as recent academic research shows. Visitors even prefer the crowd-created designs over those of famous fashion designers. This confirms that the dynamics and logic behind the model differ from those of regular fashion houses and stores.[8]

Image 1.1 My personal T-shirt design

The emergence of peer-to-peer sites has been another intriguing Internet development and business model innovation. Firms such as Airbnb, Uber, Blablacar and EatWith are overhauling the traditional business model by teaming up with consumers who are willing to rent their apartments, cars or culinary skills in return for cash. This sharing economy has created markets out of things that would not have been considered monetisable assets before. These new providers are lean organisations offering consumers the opportunity to become businesspeople on a part-time and flexible basis. They have created ingenious infrastructures that allow people to find and interact with each other, and to engage in exchange for a fee. These infrastructures or platforms render much power to these new firms that act as brokers.

The new collaborative models offer more affordable services to consumers, but are arguably more resilient too. While hotel and taxi supply are limited and any increase involves large-scale work, peer-to-peer accommodation and capacity is agile, limited only by the willingness of people to offer up their empty rooms or offer a ride. Customers are attracted to this peer-to-peer model for economic, environmental, lifestyle but also personal reasons. Key in the marketing approach are assuring trustworthy reviews, high service quality at a low price and attractive extra income for the person renting out his/her apartment or car.[9]

Several frameworks exist that can help you develop your own business model. For instance, the Business Model Canvas is a well-known and useful template.[10] Although filling in such a framework is useful, serious attention should be allocated to validating assumptions, particularly where customer interest and willingness to purchase are concerned. All too often, a validation is lacking and predictions of market demand are overly optimistic. Underestimating customer resistance can result in underestimating the efforts needed to break into the market and thus failing to make the necessary investments later. Although a smart venture capitalist or adviser should note the lack of business model validation, and call for further evidence, the failure may also go unnoticed. The result will probably be that after the new product has been developed, demand falls behind expectations and, in fact, sales never take off. Therefore, validation of the business model should be done carefully.

Although we have stressed the importance of paying customers, we should recognise that the business models of several disruptive innovators generate cash flow in a different way. They initially focus on seemingly financially unattractive market niches, but grow in terms of sales and profits over time, or complement users with sponsors, for example, advertisers sponsoring media businesses or software markets sponsoring videogame consoles. In this regard, marketing should broaden its scope by taking into account the role of users besides paying customers, and more generally, account for stakeholders besides the customer base. Otherwise certain business model opportunities may be missed.[11]

Example – Exploring alternative business models

Start-ups often adopt a certain business model, but in the process of looking for their best business opportunity, they shift to another model.[12] It is part of the experimentation stage to discover customers and validate the value of the new product for the market at large. For instance, the start-up company Inmotio began selling a monitoring device for sport teams. The product included jackets with sensors (for each player) and receivers that were placed at the four corners of a playing field to monitor several vital functions of the players and to measure their position and movement. The information gathered by the system helped coaches fine-tune individual players' efforts and team performance. However, after a while, Inmotio realised that the materials could also be rented out to teams and that the new firm could make money assisting teams by

analysing the data and selling advice and consulting. In this structure, sport teams did not have to make a large initial investment and,
as a result, were more willing to try and buy the service.

A nice YouTube video shows the product and evolution: www.
youtube.com/watch?v=DPJwGpJg478 (accessed 16 December
2016).

1.3 Products don't sell, solutions do!

Despite entrepreneurial enthusiasm, new venturing is risky, thus, most start-
ups fail; around 40 per cent fail in the first year and 90 per cent after
10 years.[13] Several reasons explain the high *failure rate*, but one is very
prevalent: many entrepreneurs are so focused on their products and product
features that they forget the customer and the problem that he or she wants to
solve. They forget that their new product or invention is bound to fail unless
it addresses a particular customer need. These entrepreneurs simply assume
rather than test the value of their product. The reason for their positive bias
is that many entrepreneurs in the process of developing their new technology
fall in love with their innovation. It is their 'baby', and as a result they are not
objective about the beauty and usefulness of the innovation. However,
customers want a product that they can understand and that works.

Entrepreneurs could seriously increase their chances by realising that
they sell solutions rather than products. To customers, products (and their
underlying technology) are *a means to an end*. Customers will be interested in a new product and technology if it solves a specific problem, and
particularly if it does this better than any other option available on the
market today.

A brief example illustrates this point. A specialist selling a high-speed
train may emphasise the technology used (e.g. magnetic fields) and say that
the new train can travel at a speed of 350 kilometres per hour, stressing that
this is a wonderful accomplishment. However, from a transportation and
customer point of view, technology and speed are less relevant – they are
relevant to the extent that they are means to an end. A customer will be
interested in the implications: the reduction in travel time, the train's safety
record and comfort, for instance. Transportation firms will wonder about
service sensitivity and reliability, among other things. In other words,
customers look for the benefits of the product and its technology. This is
true for both consumers and business customers.

Consequently, a product is best conceptualised as a 'bundle of attributes'
that offers prospective customer benefits and represents a solution to a

Table 1.1 Product versus customer orientation

	Product orientation	Customer orientation
Begins with . . .	Technology	Customer
Sees product as . . .	Focal point	As means to goal
Emphasises in discussion with customer . . .	Specifications	Attributes that deliver benefits

specific customer problem. The emphasis will be on important or so-called *salient* attributes. Each attribute generally signals to the customer how well the product can deliver a particular benefit. Salient attributes are those attributes that customers perceive as important and/or really matter in their evaluations.

The better an entrepreneur approaches his or her new technology and application using a customer perspective, the more likely customer inhibitions will be lifted and the chance of market success will increase. Because marketing and sales are business functions that put the customer first, they can help bring such a customer orientation to your start-up. Table 1.1 shows the product versus customer focus of selling a new product. In the first, the emphasis is on the specifications that follow from the technology, whereas the latter emphasises the link between product attributes and customer needs.

Consistent with the above, Peter Drucker, the 'father of modern management', identified innovation *and* marketing/sales both as any firm's core business functions:

> Because the purpose of business is to create a customer, the business enterprise has two, and only two, basic functions: marketing and innovation. Marketing and innovation produce results; all the rest are costs. Marketing is the distinguishing, unique function of the business.[14]

Our message is this: when innovating, do not forget marketing and sales; without these activities, you will have an innovation but no business.

Doing it right – Recent empirical insight

Salesmanship is central to the success of any start-up. Yet many entrepreneurs ignore it, in a large part because they have little sales experience. They, for instance, do not consider the strategic benefits to a particular customer or offer deep discounts just to make a sale.

A recent multicountry study[15] interviewing 120 start-up founders identified some of the most common mistakes. These include:

Soliciting for customer feedback too late. More than half the interviewees fully developed their products before getting feedback from potential buyers. As a result, they went to a lot of expense without knowing whether the newly developed product actually met customer needs and had market potential. Therefore, the founders' advice was to gauge customer reaction to the general product concept before developing it.

Failing to listen. Many founders' deep commitment to their course and ideas caused them to fail to listen to customer criticism. Some realised that their passion and ego had made them dismiss ideas for changes that could have increased the marketability of their products.

Offering discounts. Faced with pressure to make early sales, many founders offered price discounts which set precedents and proved impossible to reverse. It had spoiled their markets by crippling their long-term pricing power and strategy.

Selling to family and friends. Generating early sales by involving family members and friends proved to be a double-edged sword. In retrospect, founders believed those sales created a false sense of validation. Feedback from real customers is always preferred. Whereas relatives may buy from you out of sympathy and encouragement, real buyers will not – and therefore are a far more realistic test of the merit of your product.

1.4 Defining marketing and sales

Historians have argued that marketing is a combination of the words 'market' and 'getting'.[16] Two interpretations of marketing exist: (1) *marketing as a function* or set of specialised activities performed by a (group of) specialist(s) and (2) *marketing as a philosophy.*[17] The former refers to the marketing person (or department) and their activities, such as market segmentation, advertising and pricing. Two levels of marketing activities are generally distinguished: strategic and tactical activities. Marketing strategy deals with issues such as: Which customer groups to target? When and how to reach them? Tactics involve activities related to price, place, product and promotion, so for instance, determining the actual product, setting its price, developing channels of distribution for it and creating product information and advertisements. Tactical decisions should be aligned with strategic decisions and are used to detail and implement the marketing strategy.

Marketing philosophy refers to the need for firms to have a market-oriented culture which promotes all employees to *systematically* use market information and make market-informed decisions in each of its business processes. Market information can help employees understand the mechanisms underlying customer behaviour and understand the drivers of success in the marketplace against the backdrop of competitors and their behaviours. Because markets are places where customers and providers meet for exchange, customer and competitor information are important. Customer and competitor information should be collected, disseminated and used systematically. By discussing such information, a joint mindset is developed; by using the information in decision making, the organisation will *act in a market-oriented way*. A firm's marketing specialists are expected to facilitate the creation of a market-oriented culture and behaviours in an organisation.[18] If marketing performs its task well, it will create satisfied and loyal customers. Consistent with this, marketing has been defined as identifying and developing lasting customer relationships, and a marketer's time horizon is generally long term.

The customer relationships are built based on the (latent) customer value incorporated in the firm's products. By discovering the 'right' customer segment and using arguments that resonate with this group, market share can be gained. Yet, in the case of a start-up, this customer development is not straightforward. The main question is whether the newly developed product has properties that are recognised by customers and are valuable enough for them to switch from their current product and supplier to the new product and provider. The more radical the new product, the harder the relevant group of potential customers will be to discover and the more experimentation or probing of the market will be required.

The difference between *traditional marketing* and *effectual marketing* is that traditional marketing focuses on existing markets whose future can be predicted.[19] In contrast, effectual marketing embraces uncertainty and focuses on new products and markets that are hard to predict at best. While traditional marketing begins with the market and looks for (latent) needs to address, and then uses a planned and linear process to fill these needs, the effectual approach begins with the entrepreneur's new technology and product and tries, through experimentation, to find a customer group whose needs fit the new innovation's characteristics best. This process is less predictive and iterative. Additionally, as the market boundaries and logic may change, prior market information cannot be used to predict change but only to understand the current market and how things may evolve.

Finally, *sales* is the operational task involving the prioritising of and meeting potential customers as well as closing new deals. Consequently, salespeople have shorter time horizons than marketers. Sales is an important function because it generates cash flow. Sales should 'hunt' for new customers to expand business and turnover and 'farm' existing customers to ensure the firm's bread and butter. Satisfied customers are important because they may make repeat purchases and become loyal. Moreover, they may act as references to persuade other potential customers. Identifying potential customers, educating them and providing input to the firm's engineers to improve the product based on customer feedback are critical tasks.

Existing frameworks for selling typically assume that the salesperson has a ready, or fully developed, product to offer, and can focus all his or her efforts into making the sale. Although this may involve listening to the customer carefully, the goals – making sales and generating income – are straightforward. Yet, in the case of a start-up, the fully developed new product is a myth.[20] Consequently, extraordinary sales capabilities are required, such as collecting detailed information about potential improvement and redesign. Discovering those customers who most appreciate the firm's product and working with them to improve the product to a level where additional customers will accept it is an important task of the sales department/person in an entrepreneurial setting. Once this validation stage has been completed successfully, sales efforts may be stepped up and extra salespeople can be hired.[21] Then, the firm can conduct regular or traditional selling.

1.5 Beyond stereotypes

Many entrepreneurs, particularly high-tech entrepreneurs, are sceptical about the value of marketing and stereotypes about it prevail. Why? Two reasons come to mind. First, many high-tech entrepreneurs are engineers. In general, they tend to consider only the technical issues as the challenges to be met and as worth spending time on. Everything else is 'soft' or 'not concrete enough'. This attitude leads to a polarised market view and to in-group–out-group thinking. As many marketers lack technical backgrounds, they are part of the out-group.

Second, many entrepreneurs have limited understanding of marketing and sales.[22] They lack adequate knowledge about the commercial disciplines and, as a result, have a simplistic view of marketing and sales problems. They believe, for instance, that the only condition necessary for a sale is an innovative product or service. They are unfamiliar with the concepts and the importance of target market, price/quality relationships, price thresholds, distributor margins and sales promotions techniques for creating awareness and demand. They fail to see and understand that the product's unique selling points must be presented within the customer's utilisation context and frame of knowledge. Failure to see the product from the customer's context explains why it is difficult for engineers to listen to customer feedback and use it to increase the marketability of a new product.

Through discussion between the engineers and marketers or sales-people, some of these issues may be explored and resolved. Marketers are best advised to rely on social influence rather than formal claims in the persuasion process.[23] By acting accountably and showing the contribution of marketing activities to the bottom line of the start-up, marketers are most likely to persuade others, including the engineers involved, of the important role marketing plays. This may include explaining that although excellent new products might sell themselves, most new products are unfortunately far from excellent, and that excellent marketing is probably unable to sell a poor product but might be very helpful to enhance the customer benefits of moderately functioning innovations.

Marketing should be included in the list of essential tasks for any entrepreneur. Specifically, customer development as a process should complement the start-up's new product development and help identify and secure its business model.

Summary

- Entrepreneurs are people with new ideas who develop their own businesses. These business ventures are referred to as 'start-ups'.
- Radically new ideas differ from incremental innovations because they typically require substantial behavioural adjustment from customers and often change product categories, making prior market data largely obsolete.
- Effectual marketing embraces uncertainty and uses experimentation rather than prediction to find and build customers.
- A viable business model explains how and why a start-up will make money.
- Marketing and sales are important business functions to identify and develop prospective customers.

Notes

1 Guiltinan (1999).
2 Lynn *et al.* (1996).
3 Read *et al.* (2009: 1, 3, respectively).
4 Zhao *et al.* (2012).
5 Magretta (2002).
6 Ibid.
7 www.bbc.co.uk/programmes/b006vq92 (accessed 16 December 2016).
8 See www.hytencontent.com/2010/07/t-shirts-and-social-media-how-threadless-gets-it-right/#.WJBJe9xhnX4 (accessed 31 January 2017); and Fuchs and Schreier (2011), respectively.
9 www.theneweconomy.com/business/the-sharing-economy-shakes-up-traditional-business-models (accessed 16 December 2016).
10 http://en.wikipedia.org/wiki/Business_Model_Canvas (accessed 16 December 2016).
11 Dmitriev *et al.* (2014).
12 Ehret *et al.* (2013).
13 Dimov and de Clerck (2006).
14 Drucker (1985).
15 Dimov and de Clerck (2006); Fogel *et al.* (2012).
16 Kotler and Keller (2006).
17 Moorman and Rust (1999).
18 Li and Calantone (1998).
19 Read *et al.* (2009).
20 Onyemah *et al.* (2013).
21 Leslie and Holloway (2006).
22 Lynn *et al.* (1996).
23 Workman (1993); Atuahene Gima and Evangelista (2000).

Chapter 2

Identifying an application and market

Key issues

- Discuss the importance of considering several market opportunities before moving ahead.
- Understand the difference in the evaluation criteria that experienced versus inexperienced entrepreneurs use for assessing business opportunities.
- Present the bowling alley as a way of conceptualising company development over time and as a metaphor for finding your first customers.

2.1 Entrepreneurship as opportunity seeking

Entrepreneurship concerns the discovery, evaluation and exploitation of a market opportunity for a new idea or technology.[1] A *market opportunity* refers to the demand for a specific product application by a customer segment or the market as a whole. A *product application* concerns a specific manifestation of the technology and solution to a manifest or latent customer problem or irritation. It is a link between an entrepreneur's new idea or technology and the market, specifically the customers' needs. An entrepreneur's main challenge is to find the first viable product application, for which customer demand will compensate for the manufacturing and marketing costs of the new product (i.e. application).

Research shows that an entrepreneur can significantly enhance his or her success in identifying a good application by looking broadly and identifying multiple potential product applications first. This process prevents gravitation to the most obvious application. A broad search allows for a good review of the possibilities and then selection of the most viable one. However, identification of several applications prior to first entry is not common practice among entrepreneurs. In an in-depth study of a set of eight spin-offs from MIT, Shane found that *no* start-up had identified more than a single opportunity, even when better opportunities had been present and easy to spot. The entrepreneurs had simply ignored them. A larger study[2] showed similar results and confirmed that as many as 72 per cent of entrepreneurs only identified a single opportunity before moving ahead.

Inexperienced entrepreneurs, in particular, did not look beyond the first application that came to mind. In contrast, experienced or serial entrepreneurs identified several options before they made their decisions. Experienced entrepreneurs engage in a 'distant' rather than 'local' search; they search more broadly and creatively. To avoid becoming committed to an option too early in the process, they focus on developing a choice set of opportunities before evaluating and deciding. Their critical attitude and approach significantly increases the quality of ideas generated and their selection. As Figure 2.1 shows, this process involves divergent and convergent thinking.

An attractive application is characterised by low demand uncertainty (that is, it is most likely there will be customers who will be interested and buy the new product application) and high technical feasibility (that is, it can be developed in a reasonable time period and at reasonable cost).

The effectiveness of the search process resembles an inverted U. By stimulating creativity, multiple excellent options are generated, but after

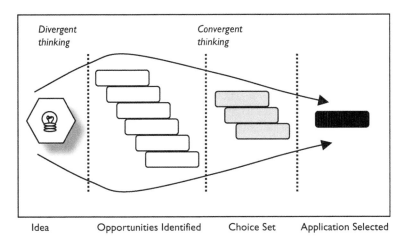

Figure 2.1 Mapping market opportunities

some time, the idea generation becomes strenuous and costly and less effective (diminishing marginal returns). Consequently, entrepreneurs should engage in search, ensuring they look beyond the obvious and stop when no further exciting new ideas emerge.

Example – Searching process for applications for electronic beam control for LEDs[3]

Imagine a new start-up focused on identifying applications for a new technology: 'electronic beam control' (EBC), using advanced liquid crystal (LC) technology to electronically, rather than mechanically, manipulate the light of light-emitting diodes (LEDs). A unique mix of light-scattering liquid crystals are integrated in a thin, transparent LC panel and placed in front of an LED to create a luminaire.[4] Specifically, the panel serves as a lens to electronically control or focus the lamp light.

The advantages of this solution include high-quality beam shaping (dynamic lighting); low maintenance (no mechanical parts); a compact form with the option of a thin, transparent panel which can be placed in front of standard LED light sources or luminaires; and easy operation (use of sensors or software).

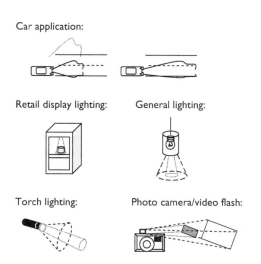

Car application:

Retail display lighting: General lighting:

Torch lighting: Photo camera/video flash:

Image 2.1 Set of market opportunities for EBC technology (adapted from van Bommel 2010)

Thinking creatively about applications for the new technology, several market opportunities can be identified, including automotive, torch lighting, photo camera flash, regular lighting and retail display lighting and so on (see Image 2.1). After a review, the entrepreneurial team decided to focus first on applications for the automotive industry, particularly in-car applications (e.g. providing the driver and passengers with better light when getting in and out of the car or for reading). The choice was motivated based on innovativeness of the market and large market size.

2.2 Evaluation criteria of the experienced entrepreneur

A systematic review of the options identified will help the entrepreneur to select the most promising alternative and will increase the start-up's chance of success. However, experienced entrepreneurs use different *evaluation criteria* to evaluate market opportunities compared with their less experienced counterparts. Table 2.1 summarises the sets of criteria that inexperienced and experienced entrepreneurs rely on.[5]

When assessing an opportunity, experienced entrepreneurs focus on the likelihood that the application can be developed successfully and that its benefits will attract prospective customers, generating money. So they quickly assess whether they can see a viable business model.[6]

In contrast, inexperienced entrepreneurs typically focus on the novelty of the idea or the newness of the technology. They are interested in how the new technology may change the industry rather than how quickly it can be developed into a viable business. They also tend to rely on their gut feeling

Table 2.1 Contrasting prototypes of novices and experienced entrepreneurs and their evaluation criteria (based on Gruber *et al.* 2008)

Novice entrepreneurs focus on	Experienced entrepreneurs focus on
How novel the idea is	Whether a customer problem
The extent to which the idea is	is solved
based on new technology	The ability to generate positive
The superiority of product or service	cash flow
The potential to change the industry	The speed of revenue generation
Their intuition or gut feel	The manageable risk
	Others in their network with
	whom to develop the venture

for selecting an opportunity rather than on anticipated revenue and earnings (that is, they fail to do a simple numbers test).

The differences between experienced and inexperienced entrepreneurs resemble the results from eye movement analyses of experienced versus novice chess players. When looking at pieces, experts produced a greater proportion of fixations on relevant pieces than did novices, who instead look at all pieces and the chess board in general.[7] Expert chess players perceptually encode chess configurations rather than individual pieces, which guides their eye movements and thinking. Like expert chess players, experienced entrepreneurs do not separately evaluate the technology, product and market, but assess the potential business model (configuration).

2.3 The particular role of marketing

While one might expect that marketing could facilitate searching for market opportunities and useful applications, conclusions are not so simple. Research by Gruber *et al.*[8] showed that inexperienced entrepreneurs with marketing knowledge found it extremely hard to avoid becoming committed to a particular market opportunity early in the process, and thus, found it difficult to come up with several ideas for product applications. So, in their case, the effect of marketing knowledge had a negative effect. However, experienced entrepreneurs with marketing knowledge did identify many more opportunities than their counterparts without such marketing knowledge (see Figure 2.2).

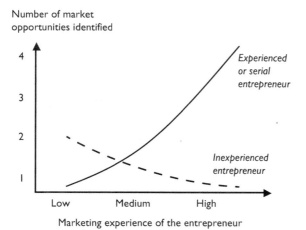

Figure 2.2 Interaction between prior entrepreneurial experience and marketing experience (adapted from Gruber *et al.* 2008)

A possible explanation for the difference is that experienced entrepreneurs use marketing in the alternative, effectual mode. As a result, they actively search for an array of possible markets and potential customer needs that fit the new technology. In the hands of an experienced entrepreneur, marketing knowledge is used to explore a new technology and application's effect on current market conditions and to explore how these may change as customers are confronted with the new modified alternative. Thus, it does not limit but actually promotes the exploration of distant and unfamiliar, yet systematic or logical options. In contrast, inexperienced entrepreneurs tend to rely on traditional marketing principles, which promote local searching by obeying existing market boundaries and product categories. Thus, inexperienced entrepreneurs become limited in their thinking.

Experienced entrepreneurs with both marketing and technical knowledge are most capable of generating many and high-quality market opportunities. Such entrepreneurs can skilfully navigate between latent customer needs and alternative technical solutions.[9] This stimulates their creativity but also allows them to optimise a product application in the process. They probe the market looking for new customers, optimise the product, and probe again. If necessary, they will move to another application and start the process again. They will continue searching until they find a useful, exciting application that fits customer needs (see Figure 2.3).

The conclusion is that effectual marketing, rather than traditional marketing, is necessary for entrepreneurs of radically new ideas to generate more market opportunities and convert them successfully into a new business. It is not linear and planned, but relies on creativity, iteration and partnering,

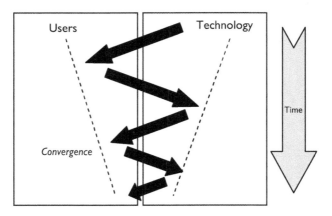

Figure 2.3 Experienced entrepreneurs navigating for the solution

Table 2.2 Comparing traditional and effectual marketing

	Traditional marketing	Effectual marketing
Market definition	Market and boundaries clear and relatively stable	Market and product boundaries challenged by new technology; discover the new delineation
Focus	Growth	Getting established
Emphasis	Exploit relationships, line and brand extension	Explore and build support; develop a network and infrastructure
Type of tools	Market research, account and relationship management, optimizing the marketing mix	Probe the market, missionary selling of technology and applications, resolving barriers
Mode	Planned action; planning cycle	Effectuation; iteration and constant leveraging of opportunities in the environment; accept coincidence

and requires seizing new opportunities as they emerge.[10] In Table 2.2, we summarise differences between traditional and effectual marketing.

2.4 Developing your bowling alley model

Moore[11] suggests using the concept of a *bowling alley* to illustrate the entrepreneur's challenge to select the first and best product application. He argues that to gain market momentum, entrepreneurs should target a niche (*the first pin* in the model) that can help open up a larger market (and preferably will lead to *a strike*). The niche refers to the first application identified and selected (e.g. automotive applications for EBC). This first application should be feasible from a technological and business point of view. Targeting this application should help secure the firm's temporary survival, but also provide information, experience and funding that will facilitate targeting and conquering other, subsequent applications and their related market segments or niches (see Figure 2.4).

Each subsequent niche (or *pin*) will require its own complete product application before its customers can consider and adopt the new technology. Yet, customers will find it much easier to buy in if the provider has

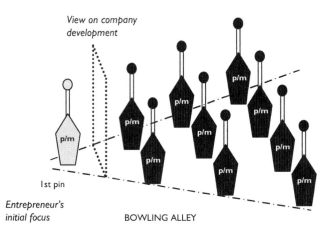

Figure 2.4 The bowling alley model (adapted from Moore 2006)

been able to demonstrate its ability to service an adjacent niche, with satisfied customers as its result.[12]

The bowling alley model is an approach for developing niche market expansion scenarios ('What would happen if . . . '). The objective should be to aim for the best pathway for a strike, that is, firm growth. Moore's key message is that an entrepreneur should develop a vision for his or her company development. The bowling alley stresses the existence of multiple product applications and the need to select the first pin carefully. By addressing the right application first, the entrepreneur can enhance its initial success which may have great impact on subsequent growth of his or her business. In a similar way, the wrong choice of the first pin or product application can seriously slow down and limit the entrepreneur's growth potential.

From experience, we know that high-tech entrepreneurs find making the right choice difficult, and more importantly, that they tend to go for the technologically most challenging option rather than develop the application that makes most sense business-wise. Because this is such an important issue we elaborate on it next.

Often entrepreneurs underestimate the risk involved and time required to turn their technology into a working prototype that can satisfy customer needs and is ready for production. They also overestimate the 'pot of gold' at the end of the rainbow. As a result, the new product application is either launched before it is ready or is never launched at all. In both cases, however, failure is the result and bankruptcy will follow. So to secure firm survival, it is better to first develop and launch a simple or feasible application. Turning this into a success will help secure the start-up's survival and allow the development of a more difficult application.

A management tool that can help you select your first application from a set of alternatives is the *real options approach*.[13] A real option is the right – but not the obligation – to undertake certain business initiatives, such as deferring, abandoning, expanding, staging or contracting a capital investment project. For example, the opportunity to invest in the expansion of a firm's factory or to sell the factory are real options. Whereas conventional financial options refer to assets traded as securities, real options refer to assets that generally cannot or are not traded.

Research and development (R&D) managers, for example, apply the real options valuation method to allocate their R&D budget among diverse projects. Because it forces decision makers to be explicit about the assumptions underlying their projections and decisions, real option value (ROV) is increasingly employed as a tool in business strategy formulation. While ROV can be used to select a single best option, it can also be used to analyse the most desirable sequence in product applications.

Huchzermeier and Loch,[14] for example, determine project value based on the five value drivers: performance, cost, time, market requirement and market payoff. Using these factors, the most interesting (highest ROV) project can be determined. Interested in the highest ROV for a sequence of applications, we extended the model of Huchzermeier and Loch by running several models after one another and assuming inter-project learning based on the fact that all projects make use of the same underlying technology. It resembles the notion of technology trajectories and Moore's bowling alley model, where a successful conversion of an application can facilitate the success of the next application. Our simulations suggested[15] that, as 'first pin' in the bowling alley, an entrepreneur should choose a simple application first, one that has relatively high technological feasibility. Successfully developing and launching the first application will result in learning spillover that increases the chance of successfully developing and marketing a more difficult application later.

This conclusion and related advice are consistent with the *principle of affordable loss*: accepting risk but limiting expenses to protect the start-up's options early in the process. The results also support the importance of thinking in technology trajectories and managing them well.

Using the extended real options approach, we also evaluated the options of the start-up from the previous example of beam control technology for LEDs. Our results confirmed that first selecting the technologically simple retail application, and then the technological challenging application in automotive, would have resulted in a maximum overall ROV for the imaginary start-up.

2.5 Managing the development of the first application

It is important to identify and collaborate with one or more *lead customers*[16] who clearly recognise the value of your new technology and/or application for their business. Lead customers are innovative and venturesome. These customers are willing to invest serious time, money and effort to help an entrepreneur develop an application and tune it to their needs.[17] Although they may cooperate because of an anticipated competitive advantage for their own business, these customers typically become involved because they love to be part of technological progress. The cooperation will be intense, allowing the entrepreneur to improve or even repurpose the technology and product application. It will help validate and bolster the customer value created by the start-up, by using the first-hand customer experience and feedback to further develop the application. However, apart from representing an excellent opportunity for finding the right product configuration, this interaction can help identify unique selling points of the new product and thus sales arguments for subsequent customers.[18]

In the process of involving customers, problems may arise, delaying completion of the new product. Although customers are generally perfectly able to express frustrations and report problems they experience, the average customer is typically incapable of identifying and voicing his or her own latent needs. Or as Henry Ford explained: 'If I had asked people what they wanted, they would have said faster horses.'[19] Another common problem is that customers may have serious doubts about their exact needs. Consequently, formulating the exact customer specifications (specs) may be very hard. Furthermore, the firm's engineers may not be able to meet all the specs. Technical problems may arise that the engineers are unable to resolve. Sometimes they will be able to get things to work but only with a tedious interface or with a feature size that is clumsy, and thus create a prototype that no one would buy and use. Similarly, the solution may be right but too costly. As a result, some concessions often need to be made. Only if concessions do not hurt the basic functionality of the new product will the application have a competitive advantage in the market and have a chance to become a success.

Even though lead customers are involved and interested in technological progress, the problem of inability to pinpoint latent needs still exists. However, compared with general customers, these leading and venturesome customers will be more capable and motivated to cooperate and work things out. Yet, a true validation will be needed to determine whether the new product is suitable for other customers in the same segment or the market at large.

Summary

- Experienced entrepreneurs focus not on new technology but on the new technology's ability to solve a customer problem and generate revenue.
- By identifying a wider range of options before selecting the first application, entrepreneurs can enhance their success.
- For a first product application, it pays to select a challenging but feasible option before aiming for a very difficult product application. This strategy is in accordance with evaluation criteria used by experienced entrepreneurs.
- The bowling alley concept offers a model of how to develop your business sequentially.
- Involving lead customers in developing your new product can increase entrepreneurial success.

Notes

1 Shane (2000).
2 Gruber *et al.* (2008).
3 Based on van Bommel (2010).
4 Hikmet and van Bommel (2006).
5 Gruber *et al.* (2008).
6 Baron and Ensley (2006).
7 Charness *et al.* (2001).
8 Gruber *et al.* (2008).
9 Griffin *et al.* (2007).
10 Read *et al.* (2009).
11 Moore (2006).
12 Popovic and Fahrni (2004).
13 Huchzermeier and Loch (2001).
14 Ibid.
15 van Bommel *et al.* (2014).

16 Note that we use the label 'lead customers' to distinguish them from 'lead users', a concept introduced by von Hippel (1986) to describe users of a technology who experience needs before others in the marketplace and who have developed their own solution for that purpose. Although leading customers also experience needs before the rest of innovator customers and are visionaries, they have not necessarily developed their own solution, but are simply open to the idea of creating such an application. However, the two concepts are clearly closely related.
17 See Coviello and Joseph (2012).
18 Ruokolainen and Igel (2004).
19 http://en.wikiquote.org/wiki/Talk:Henry_Ford (accessed 16 December 2016).

Chapter 3

Segmentation and positioning to maximise the value of a new technology and product application

Key issues

- Explain that a market is where supply meets demand and how market exchange links providers' applications of a technology to customer segments with their needs.
- Explain in detail how to identify and target the segment that benefits most from the new technology and application.
- Discuss positioning as a way to enhance the perceived value of the new product application.
- Emphasise the iterative nature of validation of the new product using first customers.
- Explain the options of technology push versus market pull.

3.1 Conceptualising the market

Although we have discussed market opportunities, we have not yet defined *the market*. Many people think that a 'market' refers to customers or customer demand. But these are only one part of the market. A market is where supply meets demand; it is the place where sellers and buyers meet and where exchange takes place. *Supply* refers to sellers competing for customers in the marketplace. *Demand* involves prospective customers trying to satisfy their needs.

Abell[1] proposed a model that is still widely recognised for conceptualising a market. He observed that in most markets, different providers and technologies exist that can satisfy particular customer segments and their needs through product (service) applications. Although customers may seem homogeneous, different groups of customers can be distinguished based on their needs and buying behaviour. Abell also noted that customers generally have not just a single need, but rather, a set of needs. Because different technologies and their applications are better at satisfying combinations of needs than are other technologies, certain customer groups will be particularly attracted by a certain technology. This explains their preference for a certain technology, product application and provider.

Abell's conceptualisation of 'the market' consists of three dimensions: (1) alternative customer groups; (2) customer needs that exist in the market; and (3) alternative technologies (see Figure 3.1).

The first dimension of Abell's model, customer groups or segments, refers to the question: *Who* are the customers? In most markets, several groups of customers exist. The second dimension addresses the question: *What* needs do these customer groups have? Although the vertical axis shows all needs, different customer groups have different sets of needs. By ordering the needs from basic to high and ordering the customer groups

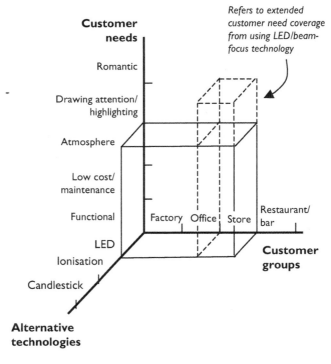

Figure 3.1 Abell's market definition and domain assessment: an example of the lighting market

from most to least sophisticated, we see a logical picture emerge. The third dimension refers to the question: *How* are needs satisfied? Different technologies and their applications are expected to be better able to address the set of needs of some segments than others. At any point in time, different technologies and systems coexist. Figure 3.1 applies Abell's ideas to the lighting market. Technologies that are available range from candles and light bulbs to LEDs. Several customer groups and a list of needs are also shown. Inside the matrix, we find the actual products (based on the technology that providers use) that customer groups buy to satisfy their specific needs. Therefore, each firm's position or domain concerns combinations of these three dimensions and may be drawn based on the scope of its activities.

This framework offers an entrepreneur an understanding of his or her market and of his or her own position or domain within this market. A product application is a specific *solution* based on a particular technology, targeted at a certain customer segment, addressing its specific set of needs.

Because customer groups, needs and technologies vary over time, the model is dynamic rather than static. Change may occur along one, two or in all three dimensions. If an entrepreneur launches a new technology and application (for example, a new online store where you can self-design your T-shirts), the technology axis is extended. If its product application also cultivates a latent need, growth via the customer need axis will occur simultaneously (e.g. a desire to make your own T-shirt design). As needs are related to customer segments, a key question is which group is most likely to recognise the importance of the new technology and switch. However, also a new customer group may emerge, that is, one that previously was not or poorly recognised due to its latent rather than manifest needs.

Doing it right – Advice on using Abell's market concept

Applying Abell's model to define your firm's market requires some practice. To come up with useful categorisations that describe the market and help to understand competitive characteristics and market dynamics, you generally have to make several attempts. Take for instance the cure market (i.e. hospitals). The technology dimension could be filled by accounting for different levels of sophistication of cure: academic/advanced, general, basic cure. An alternative approach would be: Western versus alternative medicine. Each division may be useful depending on your perspective and goal. While some people think it annoying that multiple pictures can be developed, it helps to explore opposing views and dynamics. Based on a comparison of alternative conceptualisations, a motivated choice can be made for a particular market definition.

In summary, Abell's three-dimensional presentation helps entrepreneurs conceptualise the market and understand how their new technology may change market relationships and competitive conditions.

3.2 The importance of customer segmentation

The challenge of the entrepreneur is to first identify the target customers and segment for his or her new product application. Only if the target customers like the new product concept and are convinced of the new application's superiority will developing a prototype of the application make sense. Based on these target customers' feedback, the new application can be enhanced or even repurposed, increasing the chances of success for the entrepreneur. This process is generally referred to as *co-creation*.

Deconstructing the market in more and less homogeneous customer groups or segments, based on differences in needs, is a core concept of marketing. It is referred to as *market segmentation*, but would be better labelled as *customer segmentation*. Based on the assumption that different segments have different needs and buying behaviour, positioning a new product application for a specific or so-called *target segment* can help generate customers' interest. *Positioning* implies stressing particular attributes of the new product concept to highlight its unique features compared with alternative products in the marketplace. It will emphasise the new product's strong points and de-emphasise its weaknesses. Fine-tuning the marketing efforts for the new product to this particular target segment is bound to enhance an entrepreneur's success.

The number of customer segments in a market is a function of the actual variation in customer behaviour in the market and customers' willingness to pay for a customised versus a generic product or service. However, during the launch of a true innovation, product and market differentiation generally are limited. Over time, new customer segments may evolve because of changing demand or supply. While there used to be, for instance, a market for generic deodorants, today a range of products exists for men versus women, people with sensitive skin and heavy versus light perspiration. Both supply and demand changes have stimulated the market to develop and mature over time. It has created a set of segments and products addressing specific needs.

Traditionally, marketing uses two main approaches for identifying customer segments. These will be explained first before we address identifying the best or emerging segment for a radical new product application of a new technology. These two traditional approaches are: (1) *a priori*, or deductive, and (2) *post hoc*, or inductive, identification of customer segments.

In the *a priori* approach, the entrepreneur identifies the segments beforehand, based on prior knowledge. By simply looking at a market you may notice particular groups and thus potential segments of customers attracted to certain types of products (e.g. small and large painting firms with less and more professional purchasing behaviours respectively). The quality of such segments can be tested by checking whether the customers of these segments react to product offers and related marketing efforts differently.

In the *post hoc* approach, customer segments are derived using market research. Respondents are surveyed, using a carefully worded set of relevant questions and evaluating their product preferences. Statistical analysis, particularly hierarchical cluster analysis, is then used to identify groups or segments. First, you look for significant differences in product preference, as well as other factors such as quality, advice, personal contact, warranty or service contracts, to derive the segments. Then you try to find characteristics to describe the customers of each segment (e.g. small versus large firms).

Important criteria for evaluating the quality of the derived segments include:

1   *Size*: the size of a segment is determined by the number of customers in the segment but also its spending and growth potential. A segment should be large enough to support your firm, or at least make a substantial contribution to its continuity, otherwise the segment has little value.

2   *Buying power*: the people or firms in a segment should be willing to buy but also able to afford your product or service. If they have buying power, they could be targeted and thus considered as a potential target segment. Lack of buying power makes a segment useless.

3   *Identifiability*: although conceptually one may be able to argue that a segment exists (e.g. based on product preference), it is important that the people or firms in this segment can be identified. It implies that the customers of the segment are homogeneous enough to be profiled.

4   *Accessibility*: one must be able to reach the customers from a segment. The more detailed information we have on customers' buying behaviour, the better we can implement marketing efforts for this segment. For instance, knowing which media prospective customers rely on is critical for reaching them.

5   *Stability*: the segment should be homogeneous but also sufficiently stable over time to justify your attention. When a segment is stable, a dedicated strategy can be developed that will pay off.

When marketing a new product application, you are most likely looking not for the dominant customer segment, served by the current technology, but for a less prominent or even emerging segment. This conclusion is based on a study by Christensen[2] of why large firms that once dominated certain markets (e.g. Digital, Kodak, Polaroid) were unable to successfully migrate to new emerging technology, subsequently disappearing from the scene. His conclusion was that these firms and their management became too dependent on their dominant customers. For these customers, the new emerging technology often was not a good alternative to the existing one. Compared with the existing technology, the new, emerging technology's performance was often too low on these dominant customers' most important buying criteria. As a result, the large sellers did not believe in the value of the new technology and did not launch applications based on it, even if they had mastered the new technology. Another important motivation was that the sellers' dominant customers rejected it, and that without sales to those customers, the firms would have gone bankrupt.

Consistent with the previous section, Christensen considered new technologies to enter a market 'from below' – that is, underperforming on core dimensions of the existing and dominant technology in the marketplace. He used a simple figure to illustrate his idea (see Figure 3.2). On the Y-axis, the product performance of a technology is shown, while the X-axis represents a simple time line. The bandwidth of required product performance is the area between the upper and lower boundaries of requirements. An existing (dominant) technology and a new emerging technology (technologies 1 and 2, respectively) are also shown. As the positive slopes of the market and technology lines imply, over time, market requirements increase and technology matures. While in the beginning, most new technology cannot match the quality requirements of the market, at later stages, it does appear within the bandwidth of market requirements. Finally, the technology begins to overshoot, delivering more benefits than customers desire (e.g. your computer or engine is faster than you need).

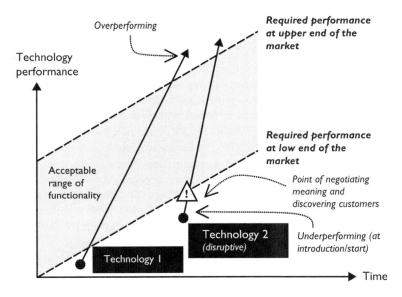

Figure 3.2 Disruptive technologies and their performance effects (adapted from Christensen 1997)

Let us now look at the point on Figure 3.2 where the new technology's (technology 2) performance becomes acceptable for some customers in the marketplace. From seriously underperforming, it slowly but surely moves towards an acceptable level of performance. This acceptable level generally concerns not the majority of customers in the marketplace, but a specific segment. Identifying this customer segment is key for the entrepreneurial marketer of a new technology and its application. It may in fact involve a new emerging segment, one that can only be found using creative segmentation strategies. Hence, one should not assume the market to be static. Over time, new technologies will reshape markets and their segments.

At the point where the new disruptive technology reaches acceptable quality levels for the new product application, the entrepreneur and his or her prospective customers will negotiate the value and meaning of the new product application, including its product categorisation.[3]

3.3 Understanding customer value

It is important that the entrepreneur looks for a customer segment that likes the unique benefits of the new application and is not (too) sensitive to its possible drawbacks. For these customers, the new product will have the highest customer value. *Customer value* concerns a customer's perceived preference for, and evaluation of, those product attributes, attribute performance and consequences of use that facilitate (or block) the customer achieving goals and purpose in his or her use situation.[4] In economic terms, customer value refers to what the customer believes she or he gains from the purchase compared with what is given up (e.g. price paid, switching costs). The concept is linked with *means-end theory*, which conceptualises products as bundles of attributes that customers use as means to reach an end state or goal. The theory emphasises considering the product in its use situation and consequences (or benefits) that goal-oriented customers will have. Because consequences can be positive and negative, customer value involves weighing gains and losses. Target customers will gain from a new technology and its application certain (functional and emotional) benefits, but will have to pay a price and may lose benefits they were used to. If the overall evaluation is negative, customers will be dissatisfied. If the overall evaluation is positive, they will be satisfied and consider the new product.

Consistent with this, Gourville[5] observes that even if a new application has merit, customers often do not like it or adopt it. He explains this based on the so-called *loss aversion theory*, an important psychological concept. First, people evaluate the attractiveness of any alternative based not on its objective, or real value but on its subjective, perceived value. They regard new benefits as gains but treat all shortcomings of the new product as losses. Because people are loss averse, these losses loom much greater than the gains involved. Second, customers evaluate the new application *relative to their current solution*. If they are happy with their current alternative and feel the extra value from the new application is small, they will not change. Ironically, many entrepreneurs conveniently forget that customers often have solutions in place that they like. Consequently, Gourville suggests that any new product should be ten times better than what existing alternatives can provide. Although this may be an exaggeration, the point is clear.

Some illustrations clarify the trade-offs involved in evaluating innovations. For instance, wind turbines may be a non-polluting source of energy, yet many people think they are an eyesore. Alternatively, screw-top caps on wine bottles do away with the problem of spoilage, but come at the expense of a less elegant drinking experience. And online grocery shopping is convenient, but you cannot check for the shelf life of the product.

3.4 Targeting using effectuation

In traditional marketing, a manager first selects the most attractive segment (e.g. based on size and growth) and then has research and development develop a new product for it. In contrast, an entrepreneur's radical new product application is the starting point, and then the target customer segment is identified and selected. So the processes of targeting and product development are flipped. If the technology and product application are new, customers first need to understand which segment will become the most interesting for the entrepreneur to target. Experimentation with customers can help to find the best match, for instance, by optimising the features of the new products for this particular segment. However, at the start, a provider can only make *assumptions* about segments and their preference, and then *test them* by meeting with customers from this segment to obtain feedback.

Figure 3.3 illustrates the effectual approach using Abell's market conceptualisation for an early provider of digital cameras. The first digital

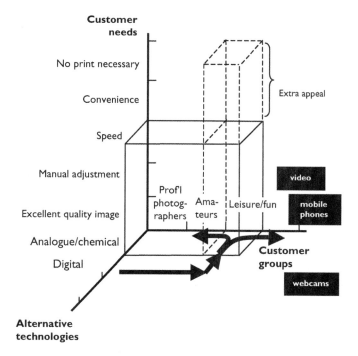

Figure 3.3 Choice of target segment: how digital cameras penetrated the market

cameras had the benefit that users could see the image quickly and share it via the web or email with friends. Costs were relatively low as film did not need to be developed in a lab and users could immediately eliminate unwanted pictures. These advantages compensated for the initial low resolution of the pictures. It was simply fun using and sharing images. Consumers therefore immediately gravitated to the new technology, whereas professional and amateur photographers, for whom resolution was much more important, were not interested at first. It was quickly obvious that the early digital cameras were best targeted at consumers, and within this consumer segment to the technology enthusiasts (i.e. the innovators). These people liked the benefits and did not mind the fairly high price or low resolution of the first cameras.

As soon as the resolution problems were resolved, camera speed improved and manual settings became available, additional segments became interested and could be targeted effectively. Soon, sales soared and prices dropped, rapidly making the product attractive even for non-technological enthusiasts, that is, the average consumers in the marketplace. As the technology matured and progressed, even dominant customers of the old technology became interested. After a while, providers of the digital technology applications decided to introduce cameras on mobile phones and extend them with video functions. As a result, the boundaries between originally separate markets began to blur.

Based on the example, we can now summarise the steps an entrepreneur can use to discover the initial target segment for the selected new product application (see Figure 3.4). First, the general dimensions of the market should be determined; that is, which technological alternatives and products exist and which customer segments and their needs they satisfy. Second, the view should be expanded to the new application. What are the unique attributes of the new product application and technology, and thus, what are the benefits it offers? In addition, which value dimensions or benefits that customers are accustomed to are less well-covered or well-served by the new technology? Third, for which segment is the value of these new benefits most important and why? Note that this response may require changing the original segments distinguished. Fourth, is there a large enough difference in value between the new application and the current product alternatives to persuade the customers of the identified segment to switch? In this evaluation, not just the benefits, and thus customer gains, should be considered, but also the losses that customers incur. Carefully make the trade-off analyses customers probably will make for themselves and determine the likelihood customers will gravitate towards your new application. Next, you should test your assumptions by soliciting actual customer feedback.

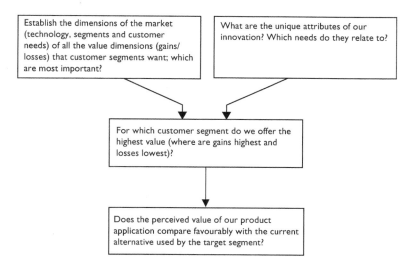

Figure 3.4 Customer value determination and targeting process

This exercise benefits from a dynamic view. The entrepreneur may consider the value the target segment will be looking for in the future. It may be that the trend is in favour of the start-up's technology and application. If so, the current value may not be sufficient, but technological progress together with the changing needs of the target segment offers future possibilities.[6]

3.5 Developing a positioning statement

The next challenge is to develop a *positioning statement* for the new product application. A positioning statement concerns: identifying the new product application's unique position (1) in the mind of the customers from this target segment, (2) by drawing on the entrepreneurial firm's unique competencies and (3) emphasising specifically the unique features of the new product application and its technology compared with competitor products and substitutes. It should result in a simple statement that can further guide the marketing efforts of the start-up. The aim is to position the product in such a way that customers of the target segment will recognise its benefits and gravitate towards it.

A useful tool for identifying the target segment and developing a value proposition and positioning statement is the framework of Figure 3.5. It offers a set of relevant questions that help you craft a solid statement.

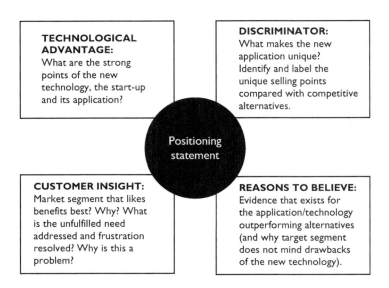

Figure 3.5 Effectual segmentation, targeting and positioning

While positioning statements are short and catchy, they are not the same as slogans or brand mantras, which generally rely on only a few keywords. Brand mantras are typically developed based on the positioning statement as part of detailing the firm's communication strategy. While a positioning statement is mainly developed for internal use, slogans and brand mantras are typically aimed at external parties. It is, however, of the utmost importance that the positioning statement explains the product's superiority using *a customer perspective*. For example, rather than selling 'a battery-powered power drill', we might conceptualise selling 'mobility to construction workers' to more effectively identify and communicate the problem solution we sell. Time spent on developing a positioning statement is time well spent. It complements initial targeting and positioning choices and facilitates the development of strong sales arguments. The statement will help the sales team to communicate the product's unique value.

The positioning statement should focus on one or more *unique selling points* (USPs) tied to attributes that the target customers think are relevant and that are substantiated by evidence. It concerns the one or two features of a product that most stand out as different from the competition and conveys its unique benefits to the consumer. The USPs and claims made should be convincing and preferably not used by competitors in their marketing.

A space already taken by the competition is not available anymore and will only buy you a *me-too*, thus not prime position. Because start-ups often sell radical product applications that customers have never seen before, clear and easily understandable statements are of the utmost importance.

Doing it right – A positioning that customers remember

Key to the exercise of positioning is that the entrepreneur chooses and develops a position that is available, credible and important to prospective customers. Availability of the position is important. Occupied positions will prevent the entrepreneur from taking a top-of-mind position, as customers resist substitution. At best, one will be labelled as copycat and second-rate in customers' memory.[7]

However, an abandoned position may be considered and adopted. For example, after first-mover Atari decided it should transform into a fully fledged computer manufacturer, the space of game computer specialist was available again. Newcomer Nintendo jumped in and became the next videogame console brand and familiar household name.

Figure 3.6 offers a framework that summarises the steps of the effectuation process of segmenting, targeting and positioning by entrepreneurial firms for discovering the customer. As explained, the sequence begins on the left-hand side of the figure with the strengths and weaknesses of the radically new product application, and then looks for a suitable or best-fitting (emerging) target segment. It involves several iterations based on market information collected in this process. Finally, the target segment will be identified and selected, after which a positioning statement can be developed to address the customers of this particular segment. This also will take several iterations, as we will explain in more detail in the following section.

3.6 Validation: initial customer feedback and iteration

By no means is segmentation–targeting–positioning a linear process. Beginning with the new product and initial target customer segment, *validation* is needed.[8] Typically, the start-up will work with its first customer(s) to develop its product, iron out problems and make improvements. Based

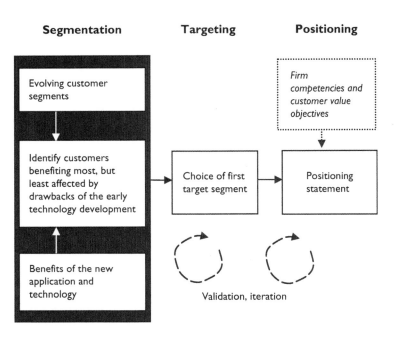

Figure 3.6 Framework for segmenting, targeting and positioning for the entrepreneurial firm

on the feedback the firm receives, it may even decide to repurpose the product in ways the entrepreneur had never imagined. When this occurs, the process of segmentation, targeting and developing a positioning statement will include several iterations. This also explains why it is important not to wait until after the new application has been developed before obtaining customer feedback. Early feedback can prevent unnecessary mistakes and investments.

The search for a useful product application – target segment connection and its iterations – illustrates how an entrepreneur should embrace market uncertainty and risk. Taking his or her idea or prototype to customers and collecting feedback is a first *litmus test*. If this feedback is positive, the initial connection has been established and attention may shift towards *further validation* with other customers from the (assumed) target segment. If these results are positive too, the entrepreneur is ready to develop the marketing mix and prospect list and scale up sales processes to build position in the target segment. With limited marketing and sales staff and small budgets, the entrepreneur needs maximum creativity to create customer awareness and positive customer associations at early stages of the start-up.

It is important to make sure that (potential) customers understand and categorise the new product correctly. Markets evolve around product categories. These *product categories* are the result of a negotiation process between sellers and buyers and allow for intersubjectivity or joint understanding.[9] They are stored in the memory as mental maps that help customers navigate in the marketplace. Generally, a hierarchical perspective is used to explain how these mental maps work. At the top, we find *abstract* categories (e.g. hot versus cold drinks; alcoholic versus non-alcoholic drinks). At the bottom are *detailed* categories (e.g. beer, speciality beer, non-alcoholic beer). Understanding whether a new technology and its application should be targeted to fit in an existing category or requires the creation of a new category is important. For example, while non-alcoholic beer has all the properties of a soft drink, it was proposed and accepted as a new, separate category. The same is true for multi-purpose vehicles (MPVs) in the car market, smartphones in the phone market and tablets in the PC market.

It should be noted that, although an entrepreneur may aim to create a new category or try to position his or her product in an existing category, the outcome depends on the negotiation process between the start-up and its first venturesome customers in the market.[10] Carefully and explicitly managing this negotiation process is important. It requires identifying and repeatedly communicating the desired (product) associations. Once customers make the wrong associations, changing them will be hard, if not impossible. For this reason, it is also important to make sure that customers who try your new product use it correctly. Bad first experiences or impressions may spread quickly through word of mouth and have a devastating effect. Even if you have objective test results that prove your new product's superiority, bad customer experiences that get out may scare other potential customers. Once such negative product associations and beliefs settle in, they will be extremely hard to change. So, managing these trials carefully and preventing negative outcomes of trials as well as ensuring correct classification of your new application product category-wise are vital. Three activities are important and should be managed well. First, identify the desired product category of your new product. Second, identify the product associations you would like to develop for your new product (and firm). Third, educate your potential customers (and the market at large) to understand your new technology, the new product and its benefits and use situation. This should also include thinking of scenarios to prevent negative associations emerging and to counter negative sentiment if it arises.

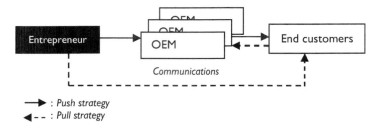

Figure 3.7 Technology push and market pull strategies

3.7 Using technology push or market pull

Many firms develop applications that involve two levels of customers: original equipment manufacturers (OEMs), who integrate an entrepreneur's product in their own products or systems, and end customers or users of the OEMs' products. Consequently, the question is: Who is our focal customer?

Technology push and *market pull* are different options in this context. Figure 3.7 illustrates these options. The first option is marketing the new application to OEMs or other direct business partners. A second option is focusing on end customers' interest and creating a demand pull for the new technology. Realising that a start-up may have multiple levels of customers can help you see more options to create inroads into a market. The idea is that by gathering interest further down the value chain, you can create pressure for intermediaries to adopt and stock the start-up's products.

It may be that your new product has important benefits for second-tier customers but it is not as attractive to the first-tier customers. An example is the digital camera. In the era of film, Kodak and Polaroid saw large retailers as their customers rather than consumers. They supplied these retailers with equipment to process photo materials and print photos. This business would suffer if these giant providers shifted to digital photography – the retailers would lose their lucrative business. This is why even when these providers entered the digital market they only offered consumers the option to put their photos on a disk, which they then could take to the retailer for prints, rather than offering consumers the option to print at home. However, firms that focused on consumer needs and began making and promoting small photo printers to allow customers their complete freedom changed the market 'bottom up' and revolutionised the industry.

Example – Push versus pull strategies for new technology

Foveon Inc. invented and designed its X3 CMOS image sensor for digital cameras. The three vertically stacked photodiodes allowed for extra data processing, offering a better photo resolution than the commonly used Bayer image sensory filter. As a result, end users were able to make better pictures and enjoy a much better photography experience. Excited about its new technology and product application, the start-up approached several large and small OEMs that were more and less integrated and with high- and low-end brands. However, these OEMs' reactions were ambivalent. Consequently, it was difficult to make inroads. Finally, the firm managed to persuade Sigma, a small manufacturer, to adopt the new technology. In fact, Sigma decided to buy the entire start-up company. Sigma then used the technology in its 2002 SD9 camera.

Now, several years later, little progress has been made. Sigma still is the only user of this advanced sensor technology. Because none of the leading digital camera brands adopted it, penetration levels remained low. In hindsight, Foveon Inc. might have been better off trying to approach and convince end users of the technology first. By building awareness and support for its technology and product application in the end-user market, the firm might have been able to create a market pull effect, which might have subsequently stimulated OEMs' enthusiasm.

Summary

- Entrepreneurs should look carefully for the segment that enjoys the benefits of their new product application most and is least sensitive to the technology's early drawbacks. Identifying and targeting this segment is an iterative process that involves making informed assumptions and validations.
- By developing a positioning statement, the fit between product application and target segment can be enhanced. This process begins with identifying the strengths (the USPs) of the start-up's application and technology.

- Make sure that customers perceive and understand the new product correctly, and develop the correct product and firm associations. Work closely with customers and listen carefully to their feedback to make sure they categorise the new product and information about it correctly. Managing this process carefully can secure and enhance your customer value.
- Customer value is not objective but subjective and includes the psychological costs associated with the behavioural change of target customers.
- To stimulate demand, entrepreneurs may approach end users, thus creating market pull for their innovation.

Notes

1 Abell (1980).
2 Christensen (1997).
3 Rindova and Petkova (2007).
4 Woodruff (1997: 142).
5 Gourville (2006).
6 Woodruff (1997).
7 Ries and Trout (1980).
8 Blank (2007).
9 Rosa *et al.* (1999).
10 Rindova and Petkova (2007).

Chapter 4

Adoption, diffusion and understanding lead customers

Key issues

- Understand the technology adoption life cycle, customer adoption and diffusion of innovations.
- Explain that for lead customers, adoption extends beyond the start-up's new product application to the technology and start-up organisation.
- The danger of chasms: discontinuities in the diffusion of a new technology.
- Reasons why customers may postpone adoption of an innovation.

4.1 The technology adoption life cycle

Because the success and failure of an innovation is so dependent on the response of potential customers in the marketplace, we need to know more about adoption and diffusion of innovations before we can proceed to discussing how to build customers for the start-up. We will begin by explaining adoption and diffusion theory.

Based on the observation that consumers and organisations have different propensities to adopt new products (services and ideas), Rogers[1] developed the technology adoption life cycle model and diffusion theory. Applied to marketing, this model postulates that if a market is confronted with the opportunity to switch to a new technology, prospective customers will have a different inclination to adopt based on their levels of risk aversion and openness to change. The propensity is assumed to be normally distributed, like most social and psychological variables (e.g. weight, IQ).

Normally distributed from more to less positively predisposed towards an innovation, the bell-shaped curve of the technology adoption life cycle model divides the whole market into five categories of potential customers. At one extreme, we find a small percentage of risk-immune *innovators* (see the left-hand side of Figure 4.1). Open to change and intrigued by the new technology and its opportunities, they want to be the first to try out the new technology and its product applications. At the other extreme, we find a small percentage of risk-averse *laggards* (see Figure 4.1, right-hand side). Hesitant to change, they avoid the adoption of an innovation as long as possible. In between are three additional groups – the *early adopters*, *early majority* and the *late majority*. These groups constitute the majority of potential customers in the market. These people have an average risk propensity and moderate attitude, and thus, an average willingness to change. Based on their moment of adoption, they can be differentiated into early and late majority, with the early adopters at the forefront of the majority. Consistent with the idea that innovators adopt first, an innovation will be adopted in sequence, from left to right.

The challenge for the entrepreneurial firm is to first obtain the venturesome innovators' interest, and then to subsequently address the

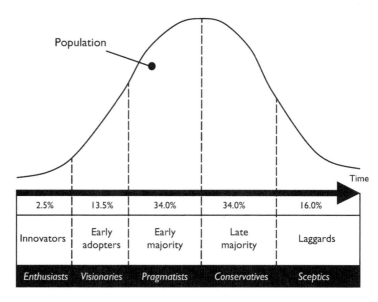

Figure 4.1 Technology adoption life cycle (adapted from Rogers 2003; Moore 2006)

needs of the other groups, taking into account their different risk propensities and attitudes. In a rather homogeneous market, this process will go smoothly, particularly if the next group follows the previous group closely and is positively influenced by its decision to change. However, markets are often heterogeneous, and serious differences between these customer groups exist, which explains the slowdown in sales growth and even discontinuation of market penetration for many innovations. Only by using special marketing tactics specifically aimed at persuading each subsequent group of customers can the firm then enhance diffusion of its innovation.

It should be noted that each group in the bell curve represents one, two or even three standard deviations from the mean. Consequently, the group structure is conceptually imposed and does not refer to clusters of people that 'naturally' exist. The groups are rather generalisations or stereotypes that marketers use to segment the market and facilitate the launch of new products and ideas, in the sense that one should try and identify innovators as a way to get the market diffusion process started. Whereas early and late majority customers are one standard deviation away, the early adopters and laggards are at two standard deviations. The innovator group is positioned at three standard deviations of the mean. Empirical research supports the general notion of the technology life cycle and its usefulness in planning the adoption and diffusion of innovations. We briefly characterise the different groups of customers in more detail.[2]

Innovators (2.5 per cent of customers). Innovators are technology enthusiasts. They are people who are fundamentally convinced and committed to new technological trends based on the assumption that, sooner or later, it is bound to lead to improvement and new benefits. They are thrilled to try any new product application. They take pleasure in learning about new technologies and mastering their intricacies. They embrace the risk and technical uncertainty involved, but are also forgiving regarding product flaws or reduced functionality of early versions of the new product. Consequently, they are always the first in the market buying the latest and greatest innovation.

From a marketing point of view, innovators are interesting because they are open to new products and willing to try them. A drawback may be that they lack money. Yet they will still influence others in the market and thus can be powerful promoters of your new product. Only with their endorsement can a radical innovation begin to resonate in the marketplace. Therefore, firms typically work closely with innovators to promote their new products and may even offer free samples to gain innovator support and their feedback.

Innovators are also the ones who negotiate the meaning of a new product and its categorisation. As an entrepreneur, you should carefully monitor this process to ensure correct categorisation of the new product and to ensure that the correct product associations are developed.

Example – The importance of ensuring correct product categorisation by customers

Dolphys Medical introduced Ventrain (see www.dolphys.com/ventrain/; accessed 16 December 2016), a new emergency ventilation device, which used a small rather than large tube. It resembled a system known as Jet ventilation. Similar to Jet ventilation, Ventrain was uniquely targeted to emergency situations remedying drawbacks of the established technology.

Aiming to further develop the new product and its market, Dolphys then made modifications which made the product also suitable for regular, non-emergency ventilation use in operating theatres. However, a problem existed. The close resemblance to Jet ventilation and initial communication/positioning that had helped Dolphys's new technology to be accepted in the first place now hindered the extension to regular usage situations. Immediate action was required to redirect people's perceptions of, and beliefs about, the firm's technology. A new marketing, and particularly communication, strategy was developed.

Early adopters (the next 13.5 per cent of customers). Like innovators, early adopters buy into new product concepts very early in the life cycle. However, unlike innovators, they are not driven by their love for innovation. They are visionary business people, but they are also rationalists. Keeping a close watch on innovators, early adopters are the true revolutionaries in business and government who want to use the radically new innovation to create serious new competitive advantage. Their expectation is that by being among the first to exploit the new technology and application, they can maximise its benefits and achieve a serious advantage over their competition. For this purpose, they are willing to ignore well-established norms, break free from existing patterns and beliefs, and rely on their own intuition and judgement.[3]

This group has an extraordinary influence on the future of the new technology because this group is the first that brings real money to the table and provides stability for the entrepreneur's turnover. Yet, there is a drawback. Based on their personal judgement and vision, each early adopter may demand some form of customisation or modification. This may prove a burden and an impossibility for the entrepreneur's resources.

Example – Differences between early and late adopters of TQM

Westphal and colleagues[4] studied the differences between early and late adopters of total quality management (TQM) by hospitals, and found that early adopters were indeed more rational while late adopters adopted because of social pressure. The early adopters were very knowledgeable and aimed to accomplish serious competitive advantages for their organisation by enhancing their product and service quality. They were able to accomplish these goals. Late adopters, however, mimicked the success of the early adopters, but often without a clear understanding of what TQM entailed. Their objective was simply to copy the behaviour of excellent peers and thus to appear to be good managers. Their objective was to appear legitimate to others. Consistent with this observation, the researchers found no effect of late adopters' adoption of TQM on their hospitals' performance or financial success.

This example illustrates the diffusion process. Innovators look for change and improvement. Early adopters act as close followers and make a careful economic value judgement. Late followers are best characterised as copycats. They give in to the new institutionalised social norm that has emerged.

Early majority (subsequent 34 per cent of customers). This group shares some of the early adopters' ability to relate to the new technology, but is even more pragmatic than the early adopters. Making up the bulk of all technology infrastructure purchases, these customers adopt because they recognise that the technology in question is being increasingly adopted by the market and becoming the standard. They believe in evolution, not revolution. They know that many innovations fail or end up as passing fads, so they are content to wait and see how other people are making out before they buy. Consequently, they look for well-established references before getting into the market and investing substantially. The early majority's influence on the institutionalisation of new social norms in the marketplace is high, higher than that of the early adopter group.

Because the early majority group makes up roughly one-third of the adoption life cycle, winning their business is key for any entrepreneur looking for substantial profits and growth. Having the right standard and features, plus an excellent price/quality ratio, are important to win this group over.

Late majority (next 34 per cent of customers). These customers are conservatives. They are pessimistic and uncomfortable about their ability to gain value from any investments in radical technology; consequently, they are hard to please. As a result of their risk-averse attitude, they are typically price-sensitive and sceptical. However, because they represent such a large group, courting this community with simpler, commoditised products or systems may still be highly profitable if costs are controlled carefully and decrease over time. Strong positive references and social norms play an important role in this prospective customer group's decision making, and thus, are important to watch and use in the start-up's marketing effort.

Laggards (final 16 per cent of customers). This final group involves people who have a negative attitude to new technology in general. They are sceptics of the worst kind. This community may be profitable for a manager who is milking declining products rather than for the entrepreneur and marketer pushing for radical innovations. The method best suited to approach this group is beyond the scope of this book.

The basic idea of the technology life cycle model is that finally all customers in the marketplace will adopt a new technology and its application. However, this is, of course, not always the case. Some customers may not be attracted to a product or prices may never come down enough to allow every customer to purchase and own the product. Still, this model of prospective customer groups with different propensities to adopt an innovation is useful to help launch a new product, and to develop and grow a market successfully. It explains the speed of adoption and thus diffusion of an innovation in a market, but also why its sales may never take off.

4.2 Penetration and diffusion

The degree of a market's adoption of a new product at a given point in time is called *penetration level*. The spreading of a new technology and its application in a market is called *diffusion*. In Figure 4.2, rapid and moderate diffusion are shown, along with postponed and accelerated take-off. The task of any entrepreneur is to avoid *chasms*, and thus to ensure

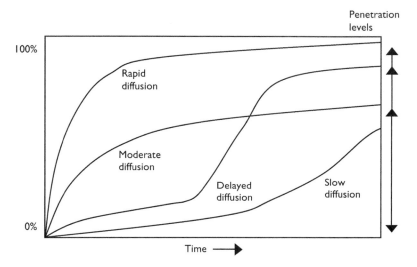

Figure 4.2 Diffusion patterns (adapted from Moore 2006)

consistent diffusion in the marketplace. Chasms are sudden slowdowns in growth of sales of a new product. They may be caused by heterogeneity of demand (i.e. customer groups available), but also by poor product performance or firm reputation which make subsequent customers reluctant.

Rapid diffusion suggests that the differences (e.g. needs and norms/values) between innovators and subsequent groups are small, therefore, the market is rather homogeneous. Moderate diffusion speed suggests moderate differences across the groups. For instance, when a market exists with many subgroups, contagion between groups may be low, explaining why the diffusion rate is low or moderate. Delayed take-off concerns a diffusion pattern characterised by a lingering curve that picks up in growth only after a certain period. If large differences exist between, for instance, the innovators and the rest of the market, the innovators will not be a good reference for the subsequent customer groups. Then, sales may only take off after the product has been changed for the needs of these other customer groups or, after that, when these groups have grown familiar with the innovation, recognising its customer value.

Although it is true that innovation attitude is a general value and very much a personal trait, this does not mean that the bell-shaped curve and its groups are the same for all innovations, and thus, for each product application. There is a variation in the distribution of people across these

;tomer groups based on product context and customers' level of product
... /olvement. Just look around you. Although young people are more
likely to be innovators than elderly people, people may be innovators for
one product but laggards for another and vice versa. Thus, it is important
for every entrepreneur to identify the innovators for his or her new product.
Innovators are the gatekeepers to any market take-off and need to be
identified and addressed first. Furthermore, the similarity and differences
between innovators and subsequent customer groups should be established
to be able to anticipate chasms and find ways to prevent or alleviate them.

4.3 Understanding lead customers

As previously discussed, for an entrepreneur, cooperating with one or
more venturesome lead customers represents an excellent opportunity for
finding the right product configuration and to make an entry with the market's innovator group. *Lead customers* are ahead of the market trend and
experience problems before other customers do. Moreover, they generally
are willing to explore ways to develop a solution to a particular problem in
cooperation with an entrepreneur or new venture. The advantage of early
customer involvement is clear: the firm generates potential customers'
interest before it invests too much time and effort in the product, and enjoys
feedback to initially test and improve the marketability of the idea and
concept.

Often a start-up will cooperate with several lead customers to probe the
market and find a product configuration for which the market segment is
large enough. As such, the lead customers are a step towards validating the
product application and its business model. Particularly if lead customers
are representative of other innovators in the marketplace the approach will
be effective. The lead customers then will be an important *reference* for
subsequent customers, and will stimulate their curiosity and interest. The
power of the reference will depend on the stature of the lead customer, its
level of satisfaction with the new product and level to which it has committed to the new technology for its business. For example, if the lead
customer is a Fortune 500 firm that has completely migrated to the new
technology, it provides confidence to subsequent buyers.

To find lead customers, entrepreneurs should look around and explore
their network. Attending seminars and trade fairs where people present and
discuss new technologies is helpful. These events draw technologically
interested parties, including lead customer prospects, therefore enhancing
the entrepreneur's chance of moving ahead and generating first and new
business.

While Moore[5] describes the customer's adoption process in terms of psychological characteristics of *individuals* rather than firms, his theory or conceptualisation can be extended to the *business customer context* too. Using a micro-institutional lens, we can transfer it to the adoption and buying behaviour of organisations. Institutional theory stresses the role of social processes and norms to explain how and why firms in an industry begin to behave similarly over time, and thus, become isomorphic. Institutions, or norms, evolve over time and help guide firm and employee actions in a specific direction. Institutions enable familiar and constrain new firm behaviour in an attempt to be efficient. Institutions are transferred using, for instance, training and routines/procedures. Yet differences between departments and disciplines cause variation in norms creating room for change, just as also individuals' curiosity may give way to exploring new options for doing business.

Despite the existence of micro-level institutional forces (i.e. normative pressure for conformity), the adoption of a new practice, product or service occurs because different professional disciplines in a firm may respond differently to innovations, which may spark change. The process revolves around the identification of an opportunity and then exploiting micro-institutional freedom called 'affordance'.[6] Specifically, it involves building support for a new idea, practice or technology within the firm by the change agent.

In the case of high-tech innovations, the initiator or change agent will generally be *a technology enthusiast*. It will be, for instance, a new product developer (chemist, engineer, etc.), head of maintenance or a plant director who sees an opportunity for a new competitive advantage. Based on his or her job, he or she actively searches for new ideas and, for this purpose, maintains relationships with expert communities where innovations are developed and new practices prevail. Receptiveness for an innovation may be higher when 'there is a sudden increase in the technical requirements for an organisational function or the social fragmentation of the expert community at the national or international levels'.[7] For example, a product developer at ASML, the world's largest chip machine manufacturer, read about a new surface treatment method invented by a small university spin-off. Excited about its potential, he introduced it in the design of ASML's next generation of chip machines. The product developer initiated the change and built support inside his organisation to adopt the new technology from the spin-off. At a later stage, it became clear that the spin-off did not meet the strict criteria to be classified as a reliable supplier to the large multinational. Quickly, measures were implemented to enhance the spin-off's professional standards, and thus, reliability as a business partner.

In summary, it is important to involve lead customers in the new product development process of a start-up. Candidate lead customers can be found in the entrepreneur's network. The chance of finding candidates is enhanced by visiting places where technology enthusiasts meet, such as fairs and seminars on new trends and technology. However, not firms but individuals create change in organisations. Relevant individuals for a start-up's new idea or product concept should be identified and approached. They can be asked for feedback and whether they have an interest in co-developing the new product and even carrying some of the development cost. Such early sales and development deals require good arrangements, but have been found to seriously enhance an entrepreneur's success. An open-minded attitude towards lead customer involvement has been found to be an important differentiator between successful and unsuccessful radical new product development by small and young technology firms.[8]

4.4 A detailed view of how innovators adopt[9]

Whereas later adopters will increasingly rely on word of mouth to make up their minds, innovators (including lead customers) adopt products based on their own, personal evaluation. This requires deliberative decision making, and thus, serious reasoning and time on the part of these customers. The matter is complex because for really new products, prior market data generally does not apply. Moreover, if marketed by a start-up, brand and firm reputation are absent too. Consequently, innovators have to look for, and rely on, alternative *sources of information* on which to base their evaluation and adoption decision.

Better knowledge about the sources of information innovators use in their decision making can help entrepreneurs better understand things they should attend to in their marketing and sales activities. Figure 4.3 shows, on the left-hand side, the sources of information innovators use to evaluate a radically new product. The adoption decision is depicted on the right-hand side of the figure. In the middle, we find a number of innovation-related characteristics that will be evaluated by the innovator. The innovator's level of enthusiasm for the new technology and application is also accounted for. This excitement is anticipated to mediate between the different information sources and the evaluation of the innovation characteristics. In the absence of 'easy product data' regarding the start-up and its new product application, an innovator will use all relevant information and signals possible. Three sources of information feature prominently: (1) reference customers; (2) characteristics of the start-up; and (3) opinions

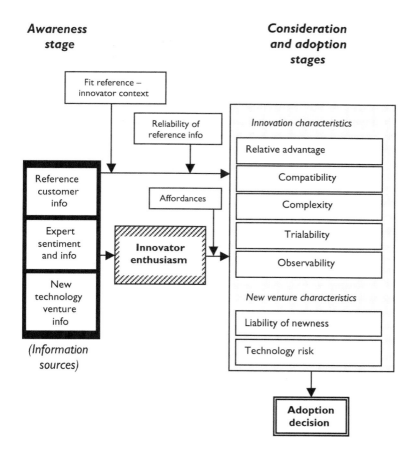

Figure 4.3 Adoption process of the venturesome customer (adapted from Wouters and Nijssen 2012)

of leading experts in the field.[10] All these sources will affect the adoption decision outcome and thus should be monitored and, if possible, managed by the entrepreneur.

Leading experts. An important source of relevant information is leading experts. Leading experts are individuals or organisations that are authorities in a certain area of technology. In the case of radical new technology, it refers to the scientific community. Leading experts help to both conceptualise and increase awareness for a technology. At early stages of the evolution of the technology, leading experts' informational influence will exceed normative effect, for example, word of mouth.

A positive sentiment from leading experts regarding a new technology and its application will enhance the innovator's enthusiasm, which in turn will increase positive factors (e.g. relative advantage) and reduce negative factors (e.g. complexity, compatibility). So leading experts' positive sentiment towards the innovation and technology of the start-up will have a positive influence on the level of innovator enthusiasm.

Because innovators are open to change, and generally are actively trying to distinguish themselves from competitors in the marketplace, they will follow leading experts closely for their views and information. Nevertheless, they will make their own evaluation rather than looking to peers or being influenced by beliefs dominant in their own industry. Innovators are not followers and have clear self-determination.

Reference customers. Reference customers typically play an important role in business-to-business marketing. Salminen and Möller[11] propose that 'firms operating in fields characterised by high technological uncertainty and investments, or trying to enter markets where they do not have established reputation, need to create references'. The successful use of a radically new innovation by a reference customer is a showcase for other potential buyers and can dispel the uncertainty of the new idea; it demonstrates that the technology and product application are operational. The previously mentioned lead customers may be used as reference (as well as any other early buyer of the innovation). The impact of the reference depends on its size, image and status, as well as on the level of commitment of these customers to the new technology (e.g. share of wallet). It will increase other innovators' confidence in, and excitement for, the new technology and product application. Reference customers positively affect the innovator's level of enthusiasm.

Apart from the indirect effect of a reference, a direct effect on an innovator's adoption behaviour is also anticipated. Particularly if there is a close relationship between the use context of the reference customer and the innovator's own business context, such direct effect may occur. In the case of excellent fit, conclusions can be translated one-on-one to the innovator's own situation.[12]

The credibility and reliability of an information source also has an impact. Information that is considered reliable and credible will be weighed more heavily than less or unreliable information. Credibility of a source increases with the level of independence. Reliability increases with quality and detail of the information. Therefore, credibility and reliability of the reference are key. It may be enhanced by offering hard evidence on, for instance, cost reduction achieved by using the new product application.

Example – Leveraging your first lead customer

The case of Sentron AG and Swiss Asulab SA, the research and development laboratory of the Swatch group, illustrates the important role of the first customer. Sentron was a small start-up that developed its first three-axis teslameter (an instrument for measuring magnetic fields) in cooperation with the Swiss Federal Institute for Technology Lausanne in 1997. It was based on a unique three-axial Hall magnetic sensor. At the same time, Asulab was looking for a good solution for a new high-end product for its Tissot brand, a watch with multiple outdoor functions including thermometer, altimeter and compass (the T-touch model).[13]

Via their university network, Asulab learned about Sentron and its innovative technology. Sentron's new vertical Hall technology allowed, for the first time, integrating instruments for measuring two components of a magnetic field on one single chip. Moreover, Sentron devised this sensor for low power, small size and high stability, which met, by chance, exactly Asulab's requirements. The fact that Sentron had sold some applications of its technology to some well-known scientific laboratories in the US helped persuade Asulab. To enhance trust, Sentron co-invested in making the necessary product changes. They reasoned that:

> [A] prestigious and visible application as a compass in a Swiss watch was much more important than an immediate profit. So, they offered the first adaptation of the existing chip for only CHF 10,000 and later the production of the test series of chips for another CHF 40,000. This just covered Sentron's costs.[14]

Start-up itself. Because many start-ups do not live beyond their initial stage, another important uncertainty for future customers exists: the chance that the start-up will not be around for future supply, warranty and service support. It may make potential customers, even the innovators, reluctant to adopt. Stinchcomb[15] coined the term 'liability of newness' to refer to this phenomenon. Adequate support from, for instance, venture capitalists and customers provides confidence in the chances for survival of start-ups. A contract with a large competitor to provide after-sales service for the start-up's products may have a positive impact too. It guarantees that service for the new product will still be available even if the start-up disappears.

The literature confirms that innovators use market and other signals to make inferences about a start-up's product quality and viability.[16] While, for example, a customer normally may rely on brands and advertising as indicators of a firm's product quality, this is useless in the case of a start-up, with its reputationless brand and minimal advertising budget. Therefore, a start-up's research-and-development spending and voluntary disclosures, as well as sales growth, are generally used as alternatives. The power of a start-up's social network and networking capabilities will also be used in this regard to assess the organisation's stability and chance of survival.

Effects of information on innovator enthusiasm

A positive evaluation of the information from the mentioned sources will fuel the innovator's enthusiasm and result in a positive evaluation of the start-up's new technology and product application. However, the degree to which the excitement seeps through from the innovator's champion (e.g. product developer or chemist) via the formal evaluation will depend on the micro-institutional freedom or affordances to break away from existing organisational norms and routines.[17] These affordances positively moderate the relationship between innovator enthusiasm and the evaluation of innovation-related characteristics; that is, the more affordances, the more likely that the innovator's enthusiasm will positively affect the evaluation of the adoption characteristics of the application and its underlying technology, and thus lead to adoption.

The affordances, and the positive influence in the buyer organisation, are important not just because a tendency to keep the status quo may exist. Often there are also sceptics in an organisation. They may actively resist the adoption of your innovation. In fact, they may even sabotage your selling of the new technology.[18] This is why it is important to know your customer; that is, to map its organisation and identify all stakeholders involved, as well as develop sales arguments for each stakeholder.

4.5 Anticipating and preventing chasms

While the bell-shaped model of the technology adoption life cycle suggests a smooth and continuous progression across customer groups, often the opposite is true. Generally, diffusion is far from smooth. The transition between two adoption segments is generally incredibly difficult because of inherent differences between these groups. Because of the psychological differences between groups, an inherent *credibility gap* exists that arises when one moves through the curve. These result in a serious slowdown in sales growth and thus development of the start-up. They are referred to as *chasms*. Apart from the need to align their message and arguments to each customer group to persuade them, entrepreneurs often need to modify their product and price to resolve the problem and get to the next stage.

In some cases, the basic affinities of the market keep customer groups relatively close together. Early adopters keep a close watch on innovators, just like late majority conservatives look to pragmatic early majority customers for guidance. Under these conditions, it is sufficient to simply update the firm's marketing as the adoption cycle progresses.

The difficulty in predicting slowdowns in growth after steep initial growth is what makes chasms so dangerous. It also explains why they may prove hard to cross for any entrepreneur. We describe two important chasms at the front end of the cycle in more detail (i.e. the early adopters and early majority chasms) to increase our understanding of and sensitivity to the issue (see Figure 4.4). We also offer advice on how to deal with these chasms.

Early adopter chasm. Many entrepreneurs are reluctant to commit to a particular market niche while their product is still under development. However, to begin making inroads and develop a relevant customer reference for new customers such marketing choices are needed. The more quickly the product's final configuration is identified, the more effective the reference will prove in attracting other innovators and the faster a transition from innovators to early adopters may occur.

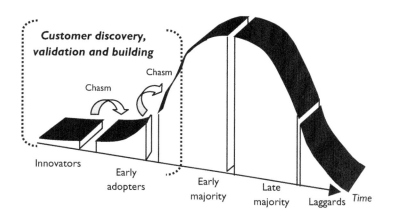

Figure 4.4 Chasms in the diffusion curve due to psychological differences (adapted from Blank 2007; Moore 2006)

Early majority chasm. The second chasm is the much-overlooked gap between the early adopters and the early majority. It is caused by the fundamental difference between these two groups. Like innovators, early adopters make their own decisions. They have a vision. While norms in the marketplace are still developing, they aim to be ahead of the majority of the market and score a technological competitive advantage for their organisation. Lack of a dominant standard may be an issue, but will not hold them back. The early majority, on the other hand, are pragmatists who only buy if the application can be readily integrated in their current processes. They generally use up substantial amounts of their budgets on consultants and other opinion leaders looking for advice. They also expect extensive references from firms in their own industry segment. Consequently, there is a serious difference or lack of fit between early adopters and the early majority, which is likely to create a widening chasm unless the entrepreneurial firm succeeds in customising its sales pitch to this pragmatic early majority.

For the early majority to be able to compare options, a product should have some competition. This suggests that alternatives should exist or be actively identified. An entrepreneur can facilitate this process by identifying substitutes and highlighting pros and cons for each product.

In conclusion, the bell-shaped adoption model with its different categories of customer groups and their different demographic and motivational particularities can help us understand how a technology diffuses in the marketplace. Differences between adopter groups explain why diffusion may sometimes suddenly increase or decrease. Awareness of these potential chasms and the underlying mechanisms enables the entrepreneur to prepare in time and take suitable action.

Example – Effectively addressing chasms

The Dutch start-up Inmotio developed a system to monitor and optimise the efforts of sports teams (see YouTube: www.youtube. com/watch?v=dq1n7IYePJI; accessed 16 December 2016). The service is composed of a set of jackets with sensors for monitoring heartbeat, perspiration and movement/direction, combined with analytic software to analyse the individual and team performances. The new firm first worked with the PSV Eindhoven (The Netherlands) and AC Milan (Italy) football teams. Inmotio had anticipated that, given football teams' large budgets, trainers would easily invest hundreds of thousands of euros in training equipment. But it soon became clear that investments in players drained team budgets and left little money for support materials. Another problem was the lack of support for science-based training methods in many clubs. Although the trainers of PSV and AC Milan were looking for science-based approaches, conservatism prevails with most football teams.

As soon as this became clear, Inmotio's entrepreneurial team considered other segments of the sports market. It decided to focus on speed skating. This sport and its trainers have been involved in scientific approaches to performance improvement for decades. The Dutch national speed skater team was enthusiastic and its endorsement helped Inmotio to enter several other sports markets.

4.6 Reasons why customers postpone or resist adoption

A final topic to discuss is the reasons for prospective customers, particularly innovators, to postpone, resist or even reject an innovation. Innovation adoption research has greatly enhanced our understanding of factors facilitating and inhibiting the adoption of innovations. It has stressed that relative advantage is a dominant driver of adoption. Nevertheless, many innovations still meet with lack of enthusiasm or resistance.[19]

The phenomenon of customers often being less enthusiastic than providers about an innovation is common. In his article on 'Eager Sellers, Stony Buyers', Gourville[20] explains that while providers typically overestimate the benefits of their new product, buyers overestimate the problems involved in adopting them. He calls this double-edged bias 'the curse of innovation' (2006: 100). It has to do with important psychological processes at both ends. Providers are overconfident that their innovation works and therefore they also like to see a need for it. They are convinced that buyers are dissatisfied with their current alternative and see their innovation as the benchmark. Customers, however, see their existing product and brand as reference points and generally tend to feel satisfied. They have a natural scepticism about new product performance; they know that many providers exaggerate product claims. Customers see a new product and weigh new benefits against switching costs and drawbacks of the new technology. Moreover, customers are loss-averse. This implies that in their evaluation, losses weigh heavier than similarly sized gains. So, the benefit of electrical cars in terms of environmentally friendly driving may not exceed the perception of reduced ease of refuelling; e-books' portability may not outweigh the decrease in durability (e.g. Amazon holding the right to remove books from your Kindle); and online grocery shopping's convenient home delivery may not be worth the disadvantage of not being able to select the freshest products.

The simplest strategy for dealing with consumer resistance is to brace for slow adoption and focus on pragmatic customers. An alternative approach is for companies to make the relative benefits of their innovations so great that they overcome the consumer's overweighting of potential losses.

Previously, we referred to customers' regular resistance to innovation. However, even more profound motivations for rejection may exist. In an in-depth study, Kleijnen et al.[21] tried to identify causes of such resistance. Based on interviews with a set of innovative customers, they came to the conclusion that resistance may be viewed as a hierarchical continuum, ranging from resistance, moving to postponement, then to rejection and to opposition, depending on both the amount and type of change and risk (antecedents) present (see Figure 4.5). If an innovation is likely to change existing usage patterns and has an economic risk, then prospective customers are likely to resist by postponing adoption (the weakest form of resistance). However, when these two factors are combined with a

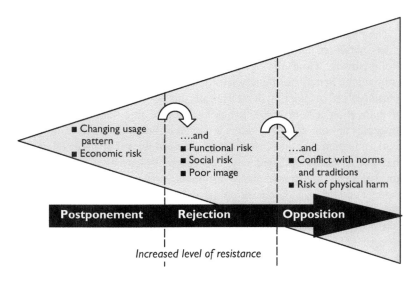

Figure 4.5 Hierarchy of innovation rejection by innovators (adapted from Kleijnen et al. 2009)

functional risk, a social risk and a poor image, they will move towards rejecting that innovation (e.g. early electric cars with very limited driving range, at least until the driving range became acceptable). Finally, when a conflict with existing traditions and norms is noted and perceived risk of physical harm added, consumers tend to move towards active opposition or even rebellion. This is the strongest form of resistance. An example is genetically modified organisms, which some groups have given the derogatory nickname of Frankenstein food.

Comparing postponement to rejection, the emphasis moves from more basic, practical concerns in the case of postponement, to more societal concerns, such as tradition and norms, in the case of rejection. Paying particular attention to these issues can help identify possible objections to an innovation at an early stage and to develop strategies to alleviate concerns that prospective customers may have.

However, in the case of customer concerns leading to active opposition and rebellion, the entrepreneur will have a hard time changing customer beliefs.

Summary

- Entrepreneurs must look for the innovators in the marketplace to make inroads. Innovators are the small percentage of people or prospects that are risk-oriented, interested in new technology and less sensitive to initial product underperformance.

- Lead customers can offer important feedback and help co-create the entrepreneur's new product application. Their feedback can seriously enhance the new product's success, with the lead user also used as an excellent reference.

- Chasms in market demand development should be anticipated. Because early majority customers are pragmatists, they may not consider innovators (i.e. technology enthusiasts) a good reference and thus postpone their adoption. Dealing successfully with chasms requires modification of the start-up's marketing and sales efforts.

- Resistance in the market against innovations is the norm rather than an exception. It should be anticipated by the entrepreneur and it requires special attention. In particular, ensuring that the new product clearly outperforms the customers' existing options is the best remedy.

Notes

1　Rogers (2003).
2　Based on Moore (2006).
3　See Westphal *et al.* (1997); Guiltinan (1999).
4　Westphal *et al.* (1997).
5　Moore (2006).
6　van Dijk *et al.* (2011).
7　Laurila and Lilja (2002: 576).
8　See Coviello and Joseph (2012).
9　This section draws on Wouters and Nijssen (2012).
10　See, for example, Popovic and Fahrni (2004); Ruokolainen and Igel (2004); Salminen and Möller (2006); DeKinder and Kohli (2008).
11　Salminen and Möller (2006: 3).
12　Simonin and Ruth (1998).
13　www.ablogtowatch.com/tissot-t-touch-expert-watch-review-the-king-of-quartz/ (accessed 16 December 2016).
14　Based on Popovic and Fahrni (2004: 931).
15　Stinchcomb (1965).
16　DeKinder and Kohli (2008).
17　van Dijk *et al.* (2011).
18　Blank (2007).
19　See Garcia and Atkin (2002); Molesworth and Suortti (2002).
20　Gourville (2006: 100).
21　Kleijnen *et al.* (2009).

Chapter 5

Competitive and market considerations

Key issues

- Explain different levels of competition.
- Define the market using a new technology.
- Discuss the importance of following a 'beachhead strategy'.
- Define network products and explain their strategic consequences.
- Offer guidelines for doing market research.

5.1 Different levels of competition

Generating intelligence regarding competitors, their products and technologies allows you to differentiate your product in a meaningful way, and thus build a better competitive position. It will also help you to anticipate competitor moves and reactions to your market entry. This is important as start-ups' limited financial resources are better spent on firm development and linking to customers than on fighting the competition.

Incorrectly, many entrepreneurs think that their products are unique and thus there is no competition. They are convinced of their product's superiority by its new features. However, even though competing products may not look or function identically, customers may still consider them alternatives. Therefore, any entrepreneur should identify and analyse alternatives and competitors carefully. If you can determine why and when some customers prefer one alternative over the other, you may begin to see patterns of competitive forces and will be able to make better marketing decisions.

So, although an entrepreneur's product may have unique features, it is bound to have some competitors. To identify these, one can simply look at products and services customers currently rely on. Whether customers think your new product is better than the existing ones on the market depends on their specific needs and how well each application is able to satisfy these needs. Often, there are multiple products in the marketplace at the same time. For instance, there are electrical and petrol hedge trimmers. By developing a detailed view of the evolving market and all product applications (based on different technologies) available, you can gain a good understanding of the market. Consumers who infrequently trim small hedges will prefer a light machine and not mind an electrical cord, whereas professional gardeners who frequently have to trim many, large hedges probably prefer, and require, the mobility of a petrol trimmer. Based on market trends, and changes in market share between competitors, underlying competitive dynamics can be identified and understood.

Marketers distinguish between different levels of competition. First, they distinguish between need and product (including brand) competition (see Table 5.1). *Need competition* refers to the fact that sales of substitutes influence each other. Substitutes look and feel different but can satisfy the same customer need. An example is teleconferencing versus air travel. Both can facilitate exchange of business information or business meetings. For instance, as teleconferencing quality increased and it became more widely available (e.g. via Skype conference calling), a serious effect on business travel was seen, particularly during the recession of 2007 and 2008. Another example of need competition is removing, versus biologically treating, polluted earth.

Similar products are interchangeable and thus also compete. This type of competition is referred to as *product competition*. One example is postal services. National postal services compete with express services. Brands operating with the same products in the same market segment also compete directly. Consequently, the actions and successes of one brand immediately affect those of the other brands. This I referred to as *brand competition*. Brand competition in the express market exists, for example, between DHL Express and services from TNT and UPS. In a similar way, KLM-Air France air travel competes with that of Emirates and British Airways, and Liebherr competes with Caterpillar cranes.

Table 5.1 Different levels of competition

Need competition	Product category	Brand competition
Screw, staple	**Glue**	Henkel, Bison, Pattex, Rubson
Air travel, postal services, email	**Postal services**	TNT, UPS, FedEx

The more similar a solution, product or brand, the more strongly they will compete. This can be explained by the simple fact that they attract the same customers.

5.2 Anticipating competitor reactions and avoiding head-on competition

It is important to identify which rivals you are most likely to take business from. The rivals who are affected most are considered 'close competitors', while those less affected are best thought of as 'distant competitors'. Close competitors generally use the same strategy (that is, they address the same customer segments with the same type of value proposition), and they share the same goals and approach.

Although these competitors may tolerate your market entry, they will probably react, for instance, with price discounts and promotions. The severity of the response will depend on whether they are attacked in their core business or not. Aiming for a firm's core business implies a direct attack and jeopardises its existence. Consequently, its management will fight back and may even react with emotional and seemingly irrational responses. To avoid this, a start-up should carefully study the competition it is up against, competitive relations and historical responses. Each individual competitor and response style should be researched and evaluated before moving in. Ignoring the simple and most obvious responses, such as temporary steep price reductions or spreading negative rumours about the new product, is dangerous. Never underestimate the effectiveness of such campaigns. Even though the rumours may be false, customers could think 'where there's smoke, there's fire'. Furthermore, customers may trust their familiar business partner and its mature technology rather than the 'outsider' with its new, unproven technology. If the campaign lasts and prevents customers from switching, the start-up's chances of success may decrease rapidly as cash flow lags behind. Developing scenarios regarding possible responses by the competition and how to respond will help to prepare. It also will increase the start-up's chance of survival.

Doing it right – Questions about your rivals that you should answer[1]

1   To what extent is each competitor satisfied with their current market position? In cases where the competitor is less satisfied with their present position, it is likely that they will follow up on

market developments quickly and will try to profit from opportunities that arise in the market. You should anticipate these moves.

2   Which possible courses of action are open to the competitor? A competitor's capability profile and resources will determine to what extent strategic options are open to a firm. Based on each competitor's strengths, some future courses of action may be plotted. If options are slim, one should expect fierce competition if a new firm enters the market.

3   Where is the competitor vulnerable? Given that a competitor cannot be strong on all items, identify weak spots that may serve as targets for competitive, strategic actions. Your new technology and application may be one, but attacking the customer segment most dissatisfied with the competitor's performance could be another.

4   How can competitive retaliations be reduced? Some segments may have lower chances than others for retaliation. For instance, firms typically see actions regarding their main market as a direct attack. Reactions may be lower in areas where the competitor's product value has already decreased or has a less dominant position.

An effective way to avoid competitive reaction is to first aim for a niche. A *niche* is a segment of the market that requires special skills and attention to sell to it successfully. As military theory[2] suggests, conquering a niche requires fewer resources than conquering an entire market. A niche strategy relies on the principle of concentration of means and is particularly useful for small firms, including start-ups. It will help achieve the necessary critical mass to succeed.[3] By pulling resources together and spending them on a particular segment, synergy can be created that can help ensure meeting a threshold level to beat competition. Of course, it makes most sense to focus efforts and resources on a niche where the entrepreneur's capabilities (technology and application) are most appreciated. This may be the segment where the start-up has, to date, made the most inroads and has most contacts. Examples of niche markets are the electrical car market, targeted by Tesla Motors for instance, and the action camera market developed and targeted by GoPro.

Simultaneously attacking several segments means spreading resources (including management attention) thinly. More importantly, attacking several segments at the same time implies opening up several 'fronts' and taking on a larger number of competitors at once. This may make the resource situation precarious and thus is better avoided. Hence, a single niche strategy is the entrepreneur's best option.

The aim for the entrepreneurial firm should be to become a market leader in a niche. A good niche is surrounded by *barriers* which make it difficult for a mainstream competitor to enter it efficiently and effectively without major efforts. For example, the luxury sports car segment is such a niche. It is difficult for regular manufacturers to make credible inroads and is thus dominated by speciality firms such as Porsche and Ferrari. Similarly, some firms have specialised in extreme cooling systems, or very large offshore construction projects that regular builders cannot address and thus avoid.

A niche strategy is particularly appropriate when the new market is supposed to grow quickly and when there are several related market segments to appeal to with the same application. The first offers the entrepreneur the chance to extend rapidly. The second offers good options to exploit other, related product applications. After the niche has been secured, it may function as a beachhead for further expansion. Building a reputation in a niche before expanding to other parts of the market offers a start-up a learning opportunity, the chance to gain maximum effect of its resources, but also the opportunity to leverage its early success effectively. Please note that this relates back to the bowling alley idea.

5.3 Change from inside or outside the industry

Porter[4] developed a useful framework for understanding industry relations and profitability. He conceptualised an industry by distinguishing between five forces: the bargaining power of suppliers, the bargaining power of customers (or distributors), the threat of new entrants and the danger of substitutes, as well as the strength of internal competition in the market between current providers or firms (see Figure 5.1). He argued that more pressure from each power would result in a reduction of *industry profitability*. That is, more internal competition would drive down prices, as would pressure from suppliers, customers, new entrants and substitutes.

Tripsas[5] analysed the conditions determining whether newcomers (new entrants) or incumbents (current providers) were the winners after a new technology was introduced in an industry. She found that in situations where the innovation caused a fundamental shift in business model, new entrants tended to do significantly better. However, when parts of the incumbent's original business model could be salvaged, the existing players stayed in power. The transition, for example, from mechanical to electric typewriters still meant a need for a large repair service organisation,

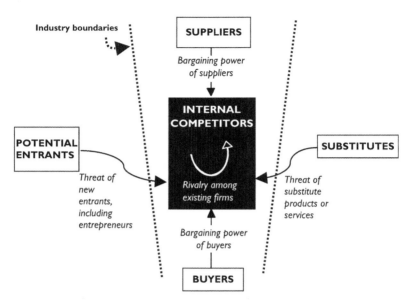

Figure 5.1 Five-forces framework (adapted from Porter 1980)

giving incumbents the upper hand. However, with the introduction of the personal computer, repair services became largely obsolete because the integrated circuit boards were no longer repaired but simply replaced.

Christensen[6] offered a simpler view of the phenomenon. He also found that radical change generally comes from outside rather than from inside an industry. Innovations generally come from substitutes and new entrants, such as entrepreneurs, rather than from incumbents (e.g. Amazon versus the traditional publishers and bookshops). The reason is that incumbents are limited by their existing beliefs, routines and customers. Engrained beliefs and routines help managers to make decisions efficiently but also limit them in responding to new trends. It breeds inertia. Further, a firm's dependence on a certain group of customers may make a firm less responsive to new technologies that are less effective, in the beginning, to serve these customers. Their customer dependence may bias a firm towards existing rather than new technology.

In conclusion, to understand whether your new technology and application have a good chance of changing the target industry and winning market share, analyse the drivers of your and incumbents' business models.

5.4 Network products and their particularities

Network products (services and systems) are products whose customer value increases as more users adopt the product, or by the presence of complementary products.[7] The customer value of a network product is determined by the product but also by the degree of acceptance in the market. It concerns two intertwined dimensions: the product's intrinsic value, that is, what the product with its particular features can do; and the product's external value, which is the number of users and complementary products necessary to unleash the product's value and enhance it. Consequently, customers' expectations about the future installed base and the resultant benefits of 'the more, the merrier' plays a critical role in their adoption decisions. We emphasise this point because radical innovations often involve changes in an industry's technical standards. When incompatible with previous standards, the aim should be to become the industry's new standard.

Network effects emanate from three sources:

1   *Direct effects.* Direct effects occur when the value of a product to any user is a direct function of the network's size or installed base. Examples are the fax machine and videoconferencing. These products can only be utilised if other users are available.

2   *Indirect effects.* This refers to the positive influence of complementary products to the value of a product. It occurs when the introduction of complementary goods increases in quantity and decreases in price as consumption of the primary product increases. Indirect network effects increase with the number of adopters because of increased attractiveness to develop and sell complementary applications or 'apps' for the primary good.

3   *The standardisation issue.* Standardisation feeds the reinforcing cycle between primary and ancillary products, based on the fact that standards make for compatibility. A standard with a large installed base will attract more complementary products and help persuade customers that they will not become locked into a poorly supported design. An example is the iPhone and its operating system versus the Android format. The question is whether Android can attract a similar stream of apps and become a major standard. Standards are just as important in business-to-business sales, for instance in shipping, software and construction. A good example of a standard introduced (too) late is Microsoft's phone operating system. Windows Phone is a series of proprietary smartphone operating systems developed by Microsoft.

It is the successor to Windows Mobile, yet incompatible with this earlier platform. Primarily targeted at the consumer market, it was first launched in October 2010. The latest release is Windows Phone 8, which launched October 2012. Market share has been small and declining with as its main client the struggling giant, Nokia. On 2 September 2013, Microsoft announced a deal to acquire Nokia's mobile phone division to better match their products, and hopefully reverse the trend. However, slipping stock prices showed that investors remained sceptical about Microsoft's chances.

The three identified sources of network effects generally are related. Figure 5.2 shows the reinforcing mechanism between the direct and indirect network effects. If indirect network effects exist and a product is launched, it is necessary to address the availability and growth of complementary products to help it succeed. If direct network effects exist, adequate efforts to ensure a *quick* and adequate adoption to build a large customer base will be necessary to unleash the new product's true value and grow a sustainable position in the market. A niche strategy will then not work and should be avoided. Instead, a rapid market penetration should be used to increase the chance of becoming the dominant standard. Customers will recognise the development of a dominant platform and reinforce the trend by gravitating to the emerging standard. So, if an entrepreneur is launching a network product, the objective should be to become the *dominant standard* as soon as possible. Involving official agencies that decide on new standards (and certification) may prove very

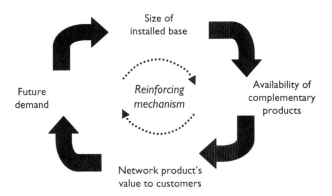

Figure 5.2 Reinforcing mechanism between direct and indirect network effects (adapted from Lee and O'Connor 2003)

useful in this regard; it can help get your standard accepted and will accelerate it becoming the new dominant standard.

Figure 5.3 shows a strategic framework for entrepreneurs who sell network products. It shows relevant antecedents and consequences that should be accounted for. Penetration pricing and bundling, that is, selling an attractive product package that is favourably priced, can stimulate adoption. It should be tied to a mass market strategy. Pre-announcement may be used to alert customers to a new network product and innovative standard that will be introduced. These strategic elements complement basic strategic logic: the product will need an adequate level of competitive advantage and early entry will give the firm an edge in building its market share and installed base. By being first, the firm's chance increases to beat the competition and get its standard accepted.

The objective of long-term profitability and customer satisfaction are dependent on (and thus mediated by) the speed of development and size of the installed base. Direct effects are also accounted for. These are relevant as different degrees of network products exist. If a product is completely dependent on 'the network', mediation will be higher than for products that also have a certain level of intrinsic value, that is, value 'outside the network'.

The framework presented in Figure 5.3 can be used by a start-up offering a network product to analyse its market and develop a strategy to accomplish its goals. It draws attention to critical elements to reach market dominance.

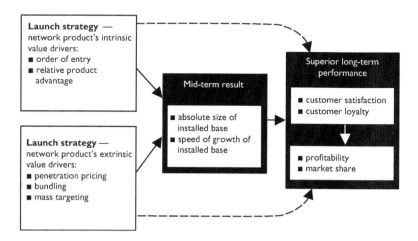

Figure 5.3 Framework linking launch strategy and performance for network products (adapted from Lee and O'Connor 2003)

Example – Failing to become the new standard will hamper start-up existence

Philips 3D Solutions, an entrepreneurial spin-off from Philips Electronics, faced the situation of a new technology standard and the challenge of dominating the future market of 3D television; 3D Solutions held a patent for 3D imaging and used a 2D-plus-Depth digital format that was an official MPEG 3D video standard. The end-user product was an LCD television with an integrated transparent display placed direct in front of the TV screen holding invisible vertical blinds. These blinds created a different viewing experience for both eyes from a distance of 10 feet. Due to this invention, the viewer no longer needed the red and green 3D glasses required by early 3D televisions to create the illusion of depth. By simply pressing a button, viewers could eliminate the vertical blinds' effect and return to 2D television images.

After first pursuing the game market and selling a number of products as gimmicks to museums and casinos, the new venture was terminated. It failed to win over enough parties to adopt its standard and thus failed to build a large enough installed base. It never made serious inroads because it failed to persuade studios and other segments to adopt the new technology. Possibly the fact that the venture only employed one new business developer, compared with some 20 to 30 engineers, explained the lack of customer development that was experienced.

5.5 Guidelines for performing market research

Market research concerns the collection, analysis and interpretation of data about the marketplace and industry at large to derive information about its size, nature and development. An industry is a set of firms focusing on the same set of activities and drawing on the same suppliers, distribution channels and customers. The market concerns the place where customers and providers meet.

Market research results in market and industry knowledge that can help make informed business decisions and reduce the *risk* involved in these decisions. Eliminating all risk is impossible for two reasons. First, it is impossible to account for all factors that may affect the outcome. Second, market research requires time and is costly, resulting in a diminishing rate of return. The optimum level of market research depends on the risk perception and attitude of the decision maker, that is, the entrepreneur. Generally, the objective is to eliminate uncertainty and consciously make a calculated decision.

Market research is easier for ongoing businesses than for start-ups with radically new products. In the case of radically new products, product categories (and in fact whole industries) may change. Technological change may cause prior market data to become obsolete. This explains why some researchers and practitioners have criticised the use of traditional market research for entrepreneurial decisions and decisions pertaining to radical technological change.[8] However, market and industry information is still required to understand the current situation. Based on envisioning the impact of a new technology and innovation, the new reality can be estimated or better 'guesstimated'; using data and arguments, the guess can be motivated. It should account for the fact that true innovative technology leads to a 'fundamental re-conceptualisation of what the business is all about that leads to a dramatically different way of playing the game in an existing business'.[9]

Two types of data collection should be distinguished: *primary* and *secondary data collection*. Secondary data collection concerns drawing on data that was collected for other purposes but that is readily available. It may be useful to your topic and question, but it was not gathered for that specific purpose and thus does not fit completely. For instance, if you have invented a new respiratory system that will be used in operating theatres, you may find it useful to see that public sources show how many hospitals exist, how many operating theatres they have and the number of operations with and without respiratory support. Sales figures of respiratory systems to hospitals may also be of interest. This data will provide a better idea of the market. Based on it, one can compute changes in the marketplace (i.e. between product groups and customer segments). Primary data collection involves new research that is focused on collecting data specifically and uniquely for a research question. For instance, let us say you want to know more about the buying behaviour of prospective customers. As this information is not available, the research question is new and unique, and specific research should be developed to answer the question. You may interview anaesthetists and employees of intensive-care units for this purpose.

Often, research involves a mix of these two types of research. You begin by collecting secondary data and complement it with primary data, either qualitative or quantitative. As a radical new product is likely to change the marketplace, you should understand the shifts that may occur. Qualitative research can help, for example, by visiting anaesthetists to learn more about their attitudes towards current systems and obtain feedback regarding the newly developed respiratory concept (e.g. factoring in the different roles people have in the decision-making process and developing an understanding of purchasing criteria used).

Primary research can be performed by the entrepreneur him- or herself, but also external help can be obtained, for instance, from a consultant, student or market research agency. Secondary data can be collected from a multitude of sources. Table 5.2 lists a number of options. The key is to check these sources and to categorise your data, for instance, using the format from an external analysis of a strategic business plan: customers, providers/competitors, distribution and general market information. It will not only facilitate analysing and interpreting the materials. It will also help identify areas where too little or no information exists yet, and thus where extra efforts are required.

Important with regard to secondary data is the *reliability of the data*. The credibility and quality of the sources is a first indication (e.g. a specialist report in *Business Week* with clear references to the sources of data is more reliable than data mentioned in a magazine or newspaper interview with a captain of industry). Another test of the quality of your data is whether other sources support it. In case of lack of consistency in data, more

Table 5.2 Sources of market information

Secondary data collection sources

- Census Bureau
- Chamber of Commerce
- Industry associations and societies
- Semi-governmental research agencies
- Banks
- Specialised market research reports
- Presentations on the Internet
- Newspapers and (industry) magazines
- Firms' annual reports

Primary data collection sources

- Market research agencies
- Own research
- Consultants
- Student projects

efforts will be needed to decide which data is more reliable and should be used.

The next step is analysing the data. It involves categorisation of customers and providers in meaningful segments or strategic groups, and computing market trends by showing annual changes. Adopting a dynamic perspective is important because you typically will be interested in how the market is and how it will be evolving. Consistent with this, the effect of different technologies (via their products) on the market should be assessed too.

Finally, an *interpretation* should be made about the effect of the entrepreneur's new technology and new product on the market. Which customer groups will be most susceptible to the new technology and product? Which providers (competitors) will be most affected, and how will the market entry of the new start-up further affect the evolution of the market? Clearly more experienced entrepreneurs, that is, those who know the market best, will be better at envisioning trends and consequences of market entry. As a result, they may be best at identifying the particular customer segment most likely to take to the entrepreneur's new product and to identify specific innovative first customers and persuade them.

The information from the two previously mentioned activities can be integrated using Abell's three-dimensional representation of the market (see Figure 3.1 and related 'Doing it right' section). The secondary market information is used to draw the basic matrix and develop an understanding of how current technologies are related to current customer segments and their needs. The envisioning of the future focuses on the growth along the technology axis and how this will alter the market. This requires new qualitative information that is used to complement and reinterpret existing products, product categories and the ways that the needs of customer groups are affected.

To summarise, it is important to collect information about the market, customer segments, competition and trends. This information enables you to understand market dynamics, including the benefits that the new product will bring to its customers. Yet, the limitations of this type of information should also be borne in mind, as it should be complemented with an understanding or guesstimation of the impact of the entrepreneur's new technology and application on product categories and industry. It helps the entrepreneur to envision the market and to develop the business case for the new venture. Insight into the overall market size, penetration levels in the segments you plan to target and price/cost levels relative to the competition can help you assess your new venture's feasibility.

Summary

- It is a real challenge to define the market for radical new products. It is difficult because radically new technology generally challenges existing market boundaries and competitive reality.
- As a start-up's resources are often limited, it is important to prevent retaliation from competitors. A niche or beachhead approach can help avoid or 'control' competition.
- Network products require a penetration strategy; the aim should be to become a dominant standard in the marketplace.
- Market research is essential and offers an understanding of the market, market trends, customer behaviour and the competition. Research complements Abell's market conceptualisation with numbers and offers input and support for an entrepreneur's vision and business case.
- Primary data from early customer involvement offers important information about the customer value of the new product and how to improve it. It complements secondary data collected about the market and its dynamics.

Notes

1 Hooley *et al.* (1998).
2 Kotler and Keller (2006).
3 Ansoff (1984).
4 Porter (1980).
5 Tripsas (1997).
6 Christensen (1997).
7 Lee and O'Connor (2003).
8 Lynn *et al.* (1996); Christensen (1997).
9 Markides (1998: 32).

Chapter 6

The customer development process

Key issues

- Explain the need for customer buy-in and a separate customer development process.
- Discuss the different steps of the customer development process and its relationship with product development.
- Explain the role of marketing and sales in the customer development team.
- Illustrate different roles customers may have in the customer development process.
- Link customer development with business model development.

6.1 The need for creating customer buy-in

If every innovation satisfied customer needs perfectly, the only marketing and sales activities needed would be creating awareness and ensuring availability. Then, customers would appear automatically on the entrepreneur's doorstep and demand the product. The entrepreneur would only have to ensure product availability to make the sale. Business growth would be instantaneous and success hard to avoid. However, innovations are usually far from perfect and entrepreneurs struggle to interest customers and persuade them of the new product's unique customer value. Based on this observation, the value of marketing for any innovation and start-up should be obvious.

Why do entrepreneurs so often design products that customers do not want? First, latent customer needs are complex and multifaceted, and customers frequently cannot express them clearly. Consequently, an entrepreneur's interpretation of these needs may be inaccurate, resulting in a suboptimal new product. Another reason may be that the start-up encounters technological problems and lacks the funds to develop a complete and suitable new product. These factors will undermine the application's quality and functionality, reducing its attractiveness for prospective customers.

Third, many entrepreneurs lack marketing and sales knowledge; as a result, they fail to understand that there is more to a product than just the nuts and bolts. They fail to understand the psychological resistance of customers to change their behaviour and overestimate the customer value of their innovation. Consequently, they also underestimate the marketing effort needed.

Some innovations may be smash hits. These typically are innovations offering great benefits, requiring minimal behaviour change, or which have an obvious target audience (e.g. a new, exciting drug for Alzheimer patients). However, most innovations are long hauls. These involve new products offering technological leaps, creating great value but requiring significant behaviour change. This is why Drucker stressed the importance of anticipating having to make major investments in the marketing of any newly developed project. He said:

> For every dollar spent on generating an idea, ten dollars have to be spent on 'research' to convert it into a new discovery or a new invention. For every dollar spent on 'research,' at least a hundred dollars need to be spent on development, and for every hundred dollars spent on development, something between a thousand and 10,000 dollars are needed to introduce and establish a new product or a new business on the market.[1]

Although you might think that he was exaggerating, recent research supports his claim.

> While the technological development associated with breakthrough innovation (BI) is truly challenging, creating markets to stimulate their use may be an even more daunting barrier to successful commercialization. Co-development partners, distribution channel agents, and ultimate users are all required to adopt new processes and to change behaviors in many cases, and the outcomes are unknown. . . . These results show that market creation for BIs may require as much time and investment as their technical development. [However,] we do not find evidence of . . . organizations' awareness of or willingness to make these investments as readily as they invest in technical development.[2]

Table 6.1 The result of different marketing efforts in combination with quality of an innovation

Technical quality of the product application	Quality of the marketing effort	Total [sum]
– –	+	–
– –	++	0
–	–	– –
0	0	0
0	++	++
++	++	++++

So, the key message is: do not skimp on marketing support and spending for the new product. By the time the new product is launched, major expenditures have been made and all possible effort should be made to recoup these costs. Reducing marketing spending will decrease rather than increase the chance that the new product will be adopted by the market.

However, spending serious money on a market launch only makes sense if the new product has potential and is not a sure failure. If the product is seriously under par, even a brilliant marketing campaign will not save it. If this happens, the research and development investments are better considered sunk costs and the project terminated. To illustrate this, Table 6.1 shows the interaction between technical and marketing quality for a new product. While excellent marketing can compensate for a less than perfect new product, it cannot salvage a very poor one. Similarly, a perfect new product may survive poor marketing support, but could have done much better if marketing had been adequate. So, the conclusion is that a firm should aim to get both its product and marketing right. A new product's quality and marketing effort complement each other.

The contribution of marketing to a start-up's new product development is in creating customers. Customers for the start-up's innovation should be discovered, the customer value of the innovation validated and a launch strategy should be developed to grow the customer base and then the firm as a whole. Although present in most new product development models, these customer development activities generally do not get enough attention. Customer development is better managed in a separate process from new product development.

6.2 New product development versus customer development

New product development is the process of creating a new product and bringing it to market. It is core to entrepreneurship. It involves several steps, including new product idea generation and selection, concept development, prototyping, market testing and launch. While at every stage of the process both technical and marketing issues co-exist,[3] most entrepreneurs (but also many large firms) limit the role of marketing and sales by leaving it till the end. They first develop the new product and then hand it to marketing and sales departments, telling them: 'Now do your best.' So '[w]hile customer input may be a checkpoint or "gate" in the [new product development] process it [often] doesn't drive it'.[4] This approach is a road to disaster. The winners at the game of new product development follow a different approach; they invent and live by a process of discovery and experimenting with customers in order to learn.[5]

Therefore, Blank[6] suggested that start-ups should complement their new product development process with a formal customer development one. *Customer development process* concerns locating a start-up's first customers, validating its assumptions and growing its business. Figure 6.1 shows the two parallel processes. We show them as complementary phenomena with serious, and preferably systematic, information exchange. While the product development process begins with a lot of ideas, one of which results in an application for launch, the customer development process begins with one or a few customers to respond to the start-up's product concept or prototype and ends, the entrepreneur hopes, with many customers purchasing the final product. Consistent with this observation we show the first process as a funnel and the latter as a reversed funnel.

While complementing product development with customer development may seem a simple and obvious extension of the process, it is not. It requires a fundamentally different way of looking at new product development. By listening to potential future customers, by going out into the field and investigating potential customers' irritations, needs and markets before being inexorably committed to a specific path and precise product specifications, the chance of success of the new product development process can be seriously enhanced. Of course, exceptions exist in the form of true technology push innovations (e.g. a new, breakthrough drug), but for most new products this applies.

A *customer development team* should be appointed to manage this customer development process. It should include, among others, the entrepreneur himself or herself and the person leading the engineering effort.

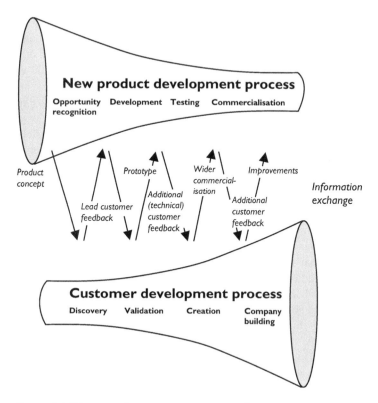

Figure 6.1 The complementary processes of new product and customer development

Preferably it will also include someone who is responsible for marketing/ sales, and thus, an individual with a product marketing or product management background. This person should be comfortable moving back and forth between customer and product development. The work of the team should help make the customer and customer needs more central and prevent the start-up from going 'all the way' only to find out later that there is no demand for the start-up's new application. After the start-up has developed a prototype and thus validated its product with first customers, the customer development team may be expanded with several people, including those responsible for moving, selling and logistics (i.e. getting early orders out).

Blank saw customer development as not just necessary, but a driving force behind a company's direction. He wrote, 'Customer Development must have the authority to radically change the company's direction, product or mission and the creative, flexible mindset of an entrepreneur.' Because of its importance, someone or a team should carefully manage it. Moreover, to prevent conflict 'this . . . team must have at its head one of the founders of the company, or if not a founder someone with an equal vote'.[7]

The dual-process approach benefits from engineers who can think like marketers, and marketers and salespeople who understand technology. That way, both processes do not stand alone but can be integrated effectively. If the two groups (new product development team and customer development team) work together well (for instance, by using some joint members as linking pins), they can open the market by identifying the most promising segment and developing a specific product configuration for it using experimentation. This will result in sales and profits that allow for company development.

Lynn et al.[8] found that success stories for new products shared several characteristics that match the process described previously. Successful firms typically had *probed* the market with immature versions of the new product as a vehicle for *learning* about the technology and customer needs. It was used to find out whether and how it could be up-scaled. This probing gave insight into the market and the market segments most receptive to the various product features, as well as about the influence of exogenous factors such as changes in government regulations. Rather than using regular marketing techniques, successful firms ran several market experiments to introduce prototypes in a variety of market segments. This research was used to probe, learn and probe again. It was their way of validating assumptions that the product developers or entrepreneur had while coming up with the new product concept.

6.3 Steps of the customer development process

Figure 6.2 shows the different stages of the customer development process, namely *customer discovery*, *customer validation*, *customer creation* and *company building*.[9] *Discovery* refers to identifying the start-up's potential customers and getting initial feedback on the idea for the innovation. *Validation* concerns working with one or more lead customers to develop or repurpose the product application. *Customer creation* builds on the success of the start-up's initial sales and uses the first customers as a reference to expand the customer base. The goal is to move beyond the group of venturous technology enthusiasts to more pragmatic early adopters. The initial sales roadmap will be further developed and fine-tuned. The final stage of

CUSTOMER DEVELOPMENT PROCESS

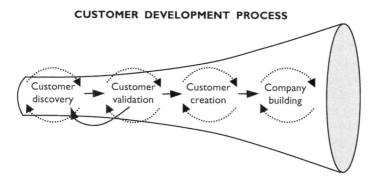

Figure 6.2 Customer development process and its stages (adapted from Blank 2007)

company building involves institutionalisation of practices and developing departments and sales and marketing capabilities. Now the search for developing and launching additional products can begin.

All four stages of the process involve various iterations, suggesting that the customer development process is far from simple or linear. This also is shown in Figure 6.2 by the feedback loops and a backward arrow accounting for potential repurposing of the start-up's technology.

Blank[10] sees the discovery stage as one of developing and testing hypotheses about the start-up's product application. It involves mapping the market, identifying the best-fitting customer segment and talking to representatives of this segment to obtain feedback. It offers a first reality check. It concerns what we have labelled 'effectual segmentation, targeting and positioning'.

The goal of customer validation is moving things forward by developing a prototype together with one or more lead customers. To find these lead customers, the entrepreneur should network. If he or she finds one who recognises the latent need and is willing to co-develop the new application, the entrepreneur could explore whether these venturous customers are also willing to share the development costs involved. Such early buy-in will help create committed partners and continuity. Next, the prototype can be presented to other potential customers to further explore its value. Their feedback will offer important information on how to enhance the initial positioning statement developed. Simultaneously, the initial sales materials, sales message and sales roadmap can be tested and improved. Channel decisions also need to be made at this point.

An indication of whether the entrepreneur has created the right product and targeted the right audience is the next stage of the customer development process: customer creation. Now, the complete launch strategy and tactics should be detailed. During this process, a transition from enthusiasts to early adopters should be anticipated. This requires detailing the customer journey and how the sales effort aligns with this. The content, form and media should be determined and the distribution channel approach, pricing and product design optimised as well. A double-digit sales growth in three or four consecutive periods may suggest that the organisation is on the right track and has been able to discover and validate its new product for its target customers.[11] Then it can add more salespeople and continue with company building.

At the company-building stage, the effectual marketing and sales are traded in for more traditional approaches. The reason is that now the customer value of the new product has been validated and the target customers are clear. Consequently, market boundaries have become clear and the product category established. Moreover, the marketing and sales roadmap has been developed, suggesting that activities can be scaled up. The challenge is to move more and more to mainstream customers or to look for new applications.

6.4 Different customer roles

Customers are, arguably, the most important external partner for small entrepreneurial firms developing major innovations. Therefore, it is important to understand the role customers can play in the new product development process of these firms. Recently, Coviello and Joseph[12] studied customer involvement in young, small high-tech firms and identified several roles customers can play. In a slightly modified form, we represent them in Table 6.2.[13] The role varies from the start-up approaching customers to give feedback on the initial idea and thus for reviewing its market opportunity, to co-developing the prototype and testing it, as well as helping to market the new product application by acting as a first customer reference or promoter to parties in its own network.

These different roles are identified on the left-hand side. They are closely related to the different stages of the new product development process. On the right-hand side are the links with the matching stages of the customer development process shown. The relationships are rather self-evident. Interesting, however, is that successful start-ups constantly solicit for customer feedback during all stages of their product development, and in this sense constantly engage also in customer development

Table 6.2 Different customer roles in a start-up's development (based on Coviello and Joseph 2012)

Customer roles per NPD stage	Customer development process stages			
	Customer discovery	Customer validation	Customer creation	Company building
Opportunity review				
Source of initial feedback	✓			
Start-up gets feedback from customer on product idea or concept; discusses product application and features and how these may help resolve current irritations/outperform current solutions.				
Source of latent needs	✓			
Start-up identifies unarticulated or latent needs when observing or questioning customer.				
Customer-based funding				
Development buyer		✓		
Start-up approaches and sells the concept as a development deal to specific lead customer(s) for R&D funding.				
Early buyer		✓		
Start-up approaches customer for an early sale, thus providing a revenue base for R&D.				
Development and testing				
Technical adviser		✓		
Start-up asks customer for technical input or specifications and technical guidance.				

(Continued)

Table 6.2. (continued)

Customer roles per NPD stage	Customer development process stages			
	Customer discovery	Customer validation	Customer creation	Company building
Co-developer — Customer engages in hands-on development and trials throughout development and testing.		✓		
Commercialisation				
Reference — Start-up asks lead customers to act as first reference and provide information on the product to other potential customers.			✓	✓
Promoter — Customer refers innovation to other potential customers and/or leverages network for sales development.			✓	✓
Feedback				
Sounding board — Firm asks customer for feedback on the concept, product or market.			✓	✓
User and critic — Customer offers extensive opinions, feedback or data on the concept, product or market.		✓	✓	✓

and validation. Moreover, after product launch, they keep looking for feedback, which serves to constantly improve the product. This implies that the whole process of product and customer development is considered an ongoing, circular process rather than a linear project with a clear end point.

We continue by identifying the marketing and sales activities per stage of the customer development process. These activities should help ensure discovering and building the customer portfolio. Figure 6.3 shows the different marketing and sales activities. Compared with the sales activities, the marketing activities are more closely related to the content of the new product development process. Sales has a boundary function. The sales activities happen more 'outside the building' of the start-up and involve searching for, approaching and working with (including educating) customers. For the customer development process to work well, it is important

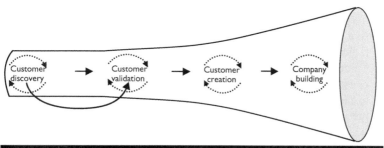

MARKETING ACTIVITIES			
• Initial market description • Initial buying behaviour analysis • Initial target segmenting • Define initial customer value	• Develop customer value and positioning • Develop initial marketing mix • Perform creative marketing • Experiment and get customer feedback • Support sales	• Build on the initial sales to create additional end-user demand and build a distribution channel • Consider how to address pragmatists • Step up awareness-building	• Move towards traditional or 'planned' marketing • Begin differentiating between marketing and sales • Continue asking for feedback • Address the majority more and more

SALES ACTIVITIES			
• Identify prospects • Obtain feedback from customers of identified and other segments • Establish problem recognition	• Look for leading customers • Explore preparedness to co-finance • Begin developing sales roadmap including prospect list and sales approach • Experiment	• Visit more customers and detail and fine-tune sales message, etc. • Begin upscaling the sales effort finalising roadmap • Educate customers, organise road shows/demonstrations	• Expand sales hunting and begin maintaining and building accounts • Expand sales force rapidly and systemise/routinise operations

Figure 6.3 Customer development process and marketing and sales activities of the customer development team

that the marketing activities support sales and that sales knowledge is used to enhance marketing decisions.

Early in the process, the different marketing and sales activities are often performed by a single person. Later, more people will be involved. How this department should evolve is hard to predict and depends on the start-up and its product. However, it is smart to regularly compare the resources spend on new product development with those invested in customer building.

Doing it right – Involving lead customers: how to identify them

For entrepreneurs, involving lead target customers in their product development is important. These customers' feedback offers a wealth of information. Many entrepreneurs think they first need a full-fledged prototype so customers can fully experience the benefits of their new product. However, reaching that stage generally involves serious investments of money and time, which both may be lost if the target customers then fail to see the merits of this new application. Therefore, it makes great sense to get quick feedback on the product concept instead. Based on the first-hand customers' critique, changes to the new product concept can be made, enhancing its value and preventing the entrepreneur from expensive mistakes.

An important question is, however, how to find these lead customers. As was mentioned, the entrepreneur should explore his or her network to identify and approach them. Firms may look for innovative customers or even lead users. Lead users have a conscious awareness of their domain-specific needs, are motivated to innovate to satisfy those needs and experience those needs earlier than others in the market.

Recent research has focused on developing scales to help identify the 'right' customers to involve in new product development (i.e. those with the unique capability to imagine or envision how concepts might be developed so that they will be successful in the marketplace).[14] We show two such scales focusing on consumers in the consumer goods industry context. The first scale refers to lead users (in a consumer setting). The second scale refers to consumers with an emergent nature (i.e. those with a unique capability to imagine or envision how concepts might be further developed for the mainstream market). This envisioning is considered to arise from a unique constellation of personality traits and processing abilities for further developing successful product concepts. It draws on and includes: openness to new experiences and ideas; an intellective self-focus, or 'reflection'; high levels of creativity; and the ability to synergistically apply both experiential and rational processing styles, among others.

It draws attention to the importance to carefully consider which customer(s) to include in the new product development of your start-up. In this regard, we have suggested in some of our previous research[15] making an explicit strategic value assessment of the customer that you will include. This assessment should address issues such as the 'lead user qualities' of the customer for gaining a particular target market, the customer's value in enhancing the strategic position of the start-up and, for instance, the financial contribution the customer can make to the development effort.

Items should be measured or operationalised using a five- or seven-point Likert scale (i.e. very much disagree to very much agree).

Domain-specific lead user scale

Other people consider me as 'leading edge' with respect to home delivery of goods.

I have pioneered some new and different ways for home delivery of goods.

I have suggested to stores and delivery services some new and different ways to deliver goods at home.

I have participated in offers by stores to deliver goods to my home in new and different ways.

I have come up with some new and different solutions to meet my needs for the home delivery of goods.

Emergent nature scale

When I hear about a new product or service idea, it is easy to imagine how it might be developed into an actual product or service.

Even if I don't see an immediate use for a new product or service, I like to think about how I might use it in the future.

When I see a new product or service idea, it is easy to visualise how it might fit into the life of an average person in the future.

If someone gave me a new product or service idea with no clear application, I could 'fill in the blanks' so someone else would know what to do with it.

> Even if I don't see an immediate use for a new product or service,
> I like to imagine how people in general might use it in the future.
> I like to experiment with new ideas for how to use products and
> services.
> I like to find patterns in complexity.
> I can picture how products and services of today could be
> improved to make them more appealing to the average person.

6.5 The relationship with the business model

Key to the customer development process is the experimentation and probing to make sure that the customer value of the entrepreneur's new product application is superior to existing solutions in the market before continuing with actual product development. The objective is to obtain information from lead customers to determine whether to abandon the idea, improve it or proceed with technical development and lead generation.

However, while product development and customer development are the operational processes, the real purpose of customer discovery and validation is development and validation of the start-up's business model. Based on customer feedback, both the product concept and target market may change. Both elements have major impact on the feasibility of the business model. Therefore, it is important to complement our view of new product development and customer development processes with a more strategic level regarding decisions of the business model (see Figure 6.4).

The information from validating product concept with lead and other prospective customers may lead to improving or abandoning the current business model. In this first case, the business model is maintained but modified and fine-tuned; it is changed with the existing product and target audience in mind. Several iterations using experimentation may be necessary before getting the model right.[16] It may involve several additional lead customers. In the case of abandoning the business model, it can be replaced by another model for the same product concept or innovation. However, it may also include a significantly modified or repurposed idea and thus a new target segment. Again, the firm will have to obtain input from prospective customers to test the idea and validate assumptions. Several iterations will be needed again.

An example of this process changing your business model is the start-up, Inmotio (www.inmotio.eu/en-GB/2/home.html; accessed 16 December 2016), which we mentioned earlier (see Chapter 4). The firm developed a system to monitor and analyse sport teams' and individual

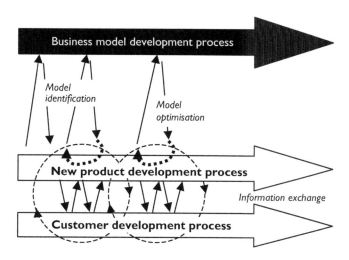

Figure 6.4 Relationship of customer and product development with business model development

athletes' performance. The Inmotio system and software combines video and statistics to report graphs and show animations. First, the firm focused on selling the equipment. However, as the system is expensive and complex, sales were slow. Next, it began focusing on leasing the equipment and helping coaches with the analyses of data collected. This reduced the initial investment required, increased customer value and stimulated adoption. Using a modular product and service structure, customers can now select the element they like and have the option to develop new extensions in cooperation with Inmotio's staff.

Thus, evolution in product and customer development processes is closely aligned with progress in the business development process; the processes are very much intertwined. Yet, recognising that all three processes are important and require adequate attention, and that none should be neglected, is key.

Summary

- Most innovations are far from perfect and require careful marketing to enhance their unique value. Without customers, there is no business. So, discovering and building customers is as important as creating the new product.

- To ensure customers for the start-up's new product application, the customer development process is best organised separately.
- A customer development team should be appointed and take charge.
- In customer development, involvement by the customer is key. Different customer roles can be distinguished.
- Customer development should help collect information for product improvement and for determining the right business model.

Notes

1 Drucker (1973: 785).
2 O'Connor and Rice (2013: 209).
3 See, for example, Cooper (1983). In this early work, Cooper showed how marketing contributes through market assessment, concept identification, concept testing, marketing plan development, prototype testing with customers, performing test markets and launch.
4 Blank (2007: viii).
5 See, for instance, Lynn et al. (1996); Leslie and Holloway (2006); Blank (2007).
6 Blank (2007).
7 Blank (2007: 38, 213).
8 Lynn et al. (1996).
9 Blank (2007).
10 Blank (2007).
11 Leslie and Holloway (2006).
12 Coviello and Joseph (2012).
13 The roles have been slightly modified to better fit the entrepreneurial setting. For instance, the customer request roles have been omitted – that is, where an existing customer approaches a firm to develop an innovation for it.
14 Hoffman et al. (2010).
15 Nijssen et al. (2012).
16 See, for example, Dmitriev et al. (2014).

Chapter 7

Developing a marketing and sales programme

Key issues

- Discuss the idea of a simple one-page marketing and sales plan to guide the effectual effort.
- Identify the three core elements of the plan: build customer value, market presence and customer relationships.
- Discuss in detail the four Ps: promotion, product, place and price.
- Emphasise the importance of creativity and social media to compensate for a limited marketing budget.

7.1 A one-page marketing and sales plan

A marketing and sales plan identifies the goals, market strategy, and marketing and sales tactics that will be used to approach the market segment best fitting the start-up's technology and application. It should help to (1) create product awareness and market presence; (2) approach and persuade prospects; and (3) clearly specify the product and its customer value. The brief plan will give structure to your start-up's marketing and sales activities and draws attention to goals and allocation of resources in a systematic but flexible way.

The most important elements of the plan should be written down. At first, it will not require more than one to two pages.[1] Later, as more assumptions have been validated and more is known about the target customers and their needs, as well as about the customer value of the entrepreneur's new product application to this audience, the plan can be expanded. Writing down the marketing decisions and actions will force the entrepreneur to specify the overall customer development goals, but also specific marketing and sales goals, strategies and tactics. The reason for the one-page document is simple. Consistent with the effectual approach, marketing and sales learning will occur through experimentation. Much of the initial plan only concerns assumptions about the market, customers and customer response to the new technology and application. These assumptions should be *printed red* in the plan and can be changed to *black or blue print* after they have been validated using customer feedback or other evidence. It will prevent confusing assumptions and facts.

The development of the plan will be an ongoing effort that is directly related to the customer development process. It begins with the aim of discovering the start-up's customers and obtaining first customer reactions to test hypotheses about the new product and its market potential. At that time, the plan will be abstract and probably include only a few actions. Subsequently, attention will shift from validation to customer creation. By including several lead customers in the start-up's product development process, assumptions about the benefits of the new product application can be further scrutinised. Working with subsequent lead customers, and using additional experimentation, the product configuration, price, distribution and sales message, among other things, then can be developed. With a more complete profile of the target customer, the marketing and sales programme can be detailed and sales scaled up.

Responsible for making this brief marketing and sales plan is the start-up's customer development team. The team should use the plan to ensure proper customer value creation and delivery by the start-up firm, create awareness and presence in the marketplace for the technology and the firm's product application, and develop a customer portfolio. Joint progress in these three domains will help develop and secure the firm's position in the market.

The one-page document should help ensure that marketing and sales *act accountably*. That is, marketing and sales should be able to show how their investments contributed to discovering and building of customers. A focus on a small set of simple marketing and sales goals may help to quantify the contribution. For this purpose, the plan should include simple marketing and sales measures. It will help the customer development team to work in a professional way and illustrate progress made. This will help build trust and support among the engineers of the start-up's organisation for the marketing and sales activities. It will help secure the necessary investments in customer development.

7.2 Content of the plan

The one-page plan should focus on creating the right *customer experience* for the start-up's new product application. It requires paying attention to three core elements: *building* (1) *customer value*, (2) *market presence* and (3) *customer relationships.*[2] Table 7.1 identifies the general content and structure of the plan, and offers a format for it.

- *Building customer value.* This refers to the fact that the start-up's product application represents a solution for customers and thus has customer value. This value should be identified and optimised. This can be done by carefully considering the different product attributes and their impact on the perceived customer value. By enhancing and highlighting the positives and reducing the negatives, customer value can be increased. The terms points of parity and difference (unique selling points) are often used. Optimisation of value will involve both technical enhancement and finding the correct framing of product claims. However, price also plays a role. Economic value refers to what a customer gains compared with what she or he has to give up. At the early stage of development there is still much that can go wrong in the value delivery process; nevertheless, excellent service can help reduce the hassle for customers and add to the customer's value experience. Therefore, managing customer expectations is an important part of the value-building process; customers understand that developing new technology and applications can be difficult. However, they like to be engaged with a provider who is in control. Finally, while a prototype may have several useful and less useful features, the optimal configuration for the target segment, and the market at large, should be determined respectively. This will help to make progress selling the product to subsequent customers, and thus, to develop the market.
- *Building market presence.* Apart from having a good product, market presence is needed for business success. The market needs to know about your technology and product to be able to act on it. This requires creating awareness for both. However, such awareness will only help your start-up if the created brand associations are positive. Hence, identifying and promoting the right associations are key activities. Building market presence includes gaining the support of opinion leaders and stimulating the press to write about your innovation, but also gaining market access. Although the Internet has made it much easier to reach out to customers and distribute your product, other

channels may be required to allow for the right installation and service support for your product. You often need to actively network to build up relationships with agents and dealers.

• *Building customer relationships*. To sustain your firm you will need a good customer portfolio. First, the right target segment for the innovation needs to be identified. It involves developing a prospect list of innovative customers and approaching these customers. Next, the contact with these potential customers can be developed, hopefully resulting in sales. By maintaining the relationship, additional sales may be obtained. The ultimate goal is, of course, to develop a portfolio of established and new customers. However, the sales task is not only towards the customer. The start-up's salespeople will need to navigate the start-up's organisation to muster support to deliver the right customer value and meet deadlines. As the new firm will need cash flow, the salespeople should try to get co-financing or secure early buy-in from customers, even if the new product is still being developed and its ultimate shape and form are still unclear.

The three elements mentioned are important for moving the start-up forward marketing-wise. For each driver, the core construct needs to be defined (customer value, market and target market, respectively), goals set (for the next period), and the means or activities for accomplishing these goals identified. Budgets should be set and allocated to the different tasks and the timing of activities should be considered and decided on. The appropriateness of timing can be accessed on a number of dimensions relative to goals, to competitors and to customers; with respect to channel cooperation, the execution of promotions and the resulting sustainable competitive advantage. The aim is to explain why the time is right for introduction and/or to discuss how to prepare customers for the new product.

The marketing activities for this period should be specified in each category. It is good to remain focused on a list with only a limited number of activities. The logic behind choices made should be written down and the consistency across activities checked. Project information should be added, also what will be done, when and who will be responsible for this. This will help ensure that the job gets done. Finally, progress should be monitored. Were activities effective, and did they help to accomplish the marketing goals in each of the three domains? The customer development team should learn from this and set new goals for the next period.

We continue with a detailed discussion of each marketing instrument, before discussing the role and activities of sales in the next chapter.

7.3 Marketing instruments

A marketer has at least four instruments to launch a new product and manage it over its life cycle.[3] These are: *product, price, place* and *promotion*. These tools are particularly useful for shaping the first two parts of the one-page marketing and sales plan: product and price can be used to establish the start-up's customer value, and place and promotion contribute to build the market presence of the start-up and its innovation (see Table 7.1).

The instrument product includes not only the physical product (or service) and its specifications, but also packaging, brand name and warranty that jointly are intended to satisfy customer needs. Price includes expectations for what customers can expect to pay, such as the list price, discount and terms of credit. At the customer end, it refers to the cost the customer will incur. Place refers to distribution and captures the various channels through which products will be made available to customers. The more easily the product can be ordered and obtained, the more convenience the customer will enjoy. Finally, promotion involves the various means of communication through which awareness and knowledge of the product are conveyed to customers and positive customer attitude is pursued; it includes traditional promotions and sales efforts, but also new, interactive media.

For services, more than four marketing instruments exist. Because services are intangible and are produced in the presence of the customer, *personnel, process* and *physical environment* are important instruments as well. Personnel refers to frontline employees – for example, sales and service employees. Their attitude and presentation are important dimensions of this instrument because they affect customer perceptions of the firm and the service it delivers. Process concerns service delivery and uniformity of service quality. During this process, service consumption takes place. Physical environment refers to the context in which the service is delivered, that is, the quality of building/room, atmosphere and other physical cues. All three extra 'Ps' affect a customer's experience.

The firm's *marketing mix* is the higher-order concept composed of product, price, place and promotion decisions. The concept of *mix* emphasises that the four factors are interdependent and need alignment. Alignment allows for synergy between these four types of instruments, resulting in extra competitive advantage. For instance, lacking unique value, commodities are generally sold at low price. They require high availability or extensive distribution to reach adequate sales levels. In contrast, speciality goods can be sold at high price levels. Because customers search out and travel to find these products, they can be offered at selected or exclusive dealers.

Table 7.1 Content of the one-page marketing and sales plan

Build customer value	Build market presence	Build customer relationships
General content		
Product features	Awareness of technology	Customer relationship management
Service	• Opinion leaders	• Prospect list
Consistency of message/experience across touchpoints	• Lead users	• Initial customer contact
Customer value	Awareness product/brand	• Relationship development
• Price	• Opinion leaders	• Repeat and up-selling
• Brand experience	• Lead users	
• Total cost of ownership	Access to distribution	
Create competition, point of reference	Educating the market	
Structure		
Definition (identify/validate)	Definition (identify/validate)	Definition (identify/validate)
• Customer value	• Market	• Target segment
• Unique selling points (points of parity and difference)	• Market size	• Target segment size
	• Brand	

Table 7.1. (continued)

Build customer value	Build market presence	Build customer relationships
Goals (this period)	Goals (this period)	Goals (this period)

• Customer satisfaction
  ○ Product
  ○ Brand experience
• Positive customer word of mouth
• Service speed/recovery
	• Awareness and associations of technology/brand
	• Distribution coverage/quality
	• Times in the news
	• Market inroads
	• Market education
		• #new prospects
		• #customers approached;
		• #demonstrations
		• #customers developed
		• #repeat sales
		• Δsales
		• Customer portfolio

Budget (this period)	Budget (this period)	Budget (this period)
Means (activities) and timing (this period)	Means (activities) and timing (this period)	Means (activities) and timing (this period)
• Product* • Price*	• Promotion* • Place*	• Sales funnel • Customer relationship management

(Continued)

Table 7.1. (continued)

Build customer value	Build market presence	Build customer relationships
Project information	Project information	Project information
• Activity/task • Responsible person • Deadline	• Activity/task • Responsible person • Deadline	• Activity/task • Responsible person • Deadline
Monitoring		
Evaluation of progress	Evaluation of progress	Evaluation of progress
• Per activity • Per objective	• Per activity • Per objective	• Per activity • Per objective

*Traditional marketing instruments.

We continue with a detailed discussion of each marketing instrument. We focus on the instruments related to customer value before moving to the instruments related to building market presence.

7.4 Product: designing a product application and product line

Product design

Product design is an important source of sustainable advantage, or as Alan Lafley, CEO of Procter and Gamble, once put it: 'Design can unlock the technological performance we build into a product and help the consumer see it, touch it. Good design is serious business.'[4]

Design refers to the actual form and shape of a product. Besides features delivering functional and emotional benefits, it also includes aspects of product appearance (e.g. aesthetics, symmetry) that influence customers' evaluations and choice.[5] As such, design has a major impact on the value of a product application for customers. Finding the right mix of features and aesthetics is particularly important. Because features often raise prices, important trade-offs are involved in adding them. Different customer segments may perceive and evaluate a design differently. Some prefer functional value, while others also are affected by aesthetic or hedonic elements.

When co-creating with venturesome customers, it is important to distinguish between core elements and more peripheral features of the design. Using a *prototype* can help in this regard. It helps to visualise the product but also experience the different product functions. The ultimate goal is to find the right mix of features for the customer and then develop it further towards a reproducible product for a broader set of customers (i.e. the market).

An interesting aspect of design is the relationship or resemblance between the new product and existing products currently on the market. Any new product will be looked at and categorised by prospective customers. If the new product's design shows similarities with familiar products, this may result in categorisation in the same product category. If the new product has different characteristics, it deviates from existing norms and expectations, which may result in confusion and, for instance, the emergence of a new category. Entrepreneurs should be aware of this phenomenon and account for it. They should decide which categorisation would serve their needs best.

Assuming that venturesome customers (i.e. innovators) are more adventurous and more knowledgeable, some rationalisation of product design may be required to persuade early adopters and the rest of the market to adopt the new product too. Research shows that expert customers have more imagination and thus may link a futuristic or different product design to their needs more easily than less knowledgeable customers. To prevent chasms, special attention to product design will be required.

Products as bundles of attributes

Products are best conceptualised as bundles of attributes. *Salient attributes* are features that customers think are important because they offer benefits. It is important to learn about these salient attributes and their threshold values, or minimal requirement levels. Generally, customers will insist that a new product offers the benefits of the current technology and product(s) available, and also offer something extra.

In Table 7.2, we show how the first digital cameras offered a fair picture quality but superior flexibility to teenagers. As a result, teenagers' attitudes towards these cameras were more favourable, stimulating demand for the new product. Specifically, the table shows, on the left-hand side, a number of salient attributes. The average weight or importance of each attribute, called *belief*, is shown (such a score can be found using market research, for example, a survey). Finally, we see the average rating of the two product alternatives (i.e. the current and new product). Because the overall score (belief × rating) for the new product is more favourable, this product is considered superior and will be chosen and purchased over the old camera type.

Table 7.2 Illustration of the product attribute model for the first digital camera and teenager segment

Teenagers' evaluations:		Disposable camera	First digital camera
	Beliefs (importance, 1–5)	**Evaluation (1–10)**	**Evaluation (1–10)**
Salient attributes:			
Picture quality	4	8 (Good)	6 (Fair)
Flexibility	3	2 (No/low)	9 (Excellent)
Ability to forward pictures to friends	3	3 (Low)	7 (High)
Total score*		47	72

*Total score $= \sum_{i=1}^{n}$ (Beliefs × Evaluation)

Another relevant product concept is the distinction between core, extended and *augmented product*. The core product is the generic, tangible product that the customer experiences. The extended product is the core product but with additional physical and design features. The augmented product refers to the whole, potential product. It includes all current and future features, elements and services that make the product more valuable and thus are potentially compelling to customers. For example, if a personal computer is the core product, then the extended product includes software applications and peripheral devices such as a mouse, keyboard and printer. The augmented product includes all possible options such as extra warranty with home servicing, automatic software updates, lease options and so on.

While customer discovery and validation address the question of what the start-up's core product should be and entail, the augmented product may be highly relevant to the question of how the firm will make money or extend its business. Particularly if an entrepreneur's new product is used by customers in their manufacturing processes, service support will be an important customer requirement. Lack of service support may reduce the value of the product, and prevent customers from considering and adopting it. The business case for the new product should recognise this aspect and ensure an overall product value that will be appreciated and help customers accomplish the extra competitive advantage they are looking for.

Product line issues

Although venturesome customers (i.e. innovators) may be attracted to a new product and its design, its quality generally needs to be improved rapidly for a start-up to attract the more pragmatic early adopters and early majority in the market. These customer groups only move forward when risk is low and when advantages clearly outweigh costs. Thus, optimising your product soon after its introduction is of the utmost importance. Based on the feedback of these pragmatists, you may be able to trim unnecessary product features or enhance features considered useful. In the process, you may decide to launch a new version (new product 2.0), thus creating a *product line*. Adding a similar product with more or fewer features is considered upward and downward stretching, respectively.

A product line is a group of related products defined by their functions and customer market, forming a line. For instance, the variety of coffee offered at a café. A product line can be described using three dimensions: length, breadth and depth. Length refers to the number of similar products carried to cater to the firm's customers (e.g. coffee, espresso, cappuccino, latte). The more variety, the longer the line. Depth refers to the level of variation in a product line (e.g. size, flavours or other distinctive factors). Breadth refers to the total number of product lines of a firm (e.g. product lines of juices and pastries can also be found at a café).

Product line design is a central issue in marketing. By creating the ideal product for each customer segment, a firm can cater to specific variations in customer needs, and best satisfy different customer groups. It allows the firm to charge premium prices for these products while satisfying the customers. However, fixed costs associated with adding products to the product line and potential cannibalisation on the demand for the existing products may reduce the total profit to the start-up from this product line. The trade-offs between these factors determine which products are best developed and offered and at what prices. For most start-ups, the best solution probably is to limit customer choice and thus their product line.

The basis for a product line are the attributes from which a product is made. Using these attributes, one optimal configuration can be created for most customers in the marketplace, but also different product configurations can be developed to address different segments. Showing the different configurations to these target customers, and varying the set and levels of attributes, permits assessment of their willingness to pay for these more customised products. Yet again, for start-ups, this is valuable information but keeping their product line simple is probably the best advice.

Example – GoPro's product line development

In 2002, a brand-new camera maker emerged: GoPro. Inventor Nick Woodman got the idea for the small action-camera during a long vacation, after his first start-up on online gaming had crashed. The aim was to make cameras for surfers. The original, 2.5-by-3-inch product shot 35mm film. It debuted at an action-sports trade show in 2004. The 35mm camera (model #001) became available on 13 April 2005, and came with a clear case with quick release, a camera strap, a ski glove adapter lash and a roll of 24 exposure Kodak 400 film.

New models, in rapid succession, incorporated digital stills, video, audio and every megapixel and memory upgrade the marketplace came up with. The Digital HERO 1 was released in 2006 (Model: SQ907 mini-cam) had a 640×460 camera and shot VGA definition 320×240 (10fps) video for a maximum of 10 seconds. The Digital HERO 3 and 5 were released in 2007 and 2008, respectively, and had a 3- and 5-megapixel camera. The HERO 2 was launched on

24 October 2011. It had an 11 MP image sensor, improved low-light capability and recorded at up to 120 frames per second. It was sold with three different accessory packages as the Outdoor, Motorsports and Surf Editions.

In late 2012, GoPro announced the HERO 3 line of cameras. These new cameras came in three editions: black, silver and white. Thirty per cent smaller and lighter than the previous generations (HERO 1 and HERO 2 were physically identical), new versions of accessories were needed. In September 2014, GoPro launched its new HERO 4 line of cameras, which replaced their respective HERO 3 + predecessors. They included three new cameras: at entry level, the HERO, selling at $129, at the mid-level HERO 4 silver (with integrated LCD) selling at $399 and at the top, the flagship HERO 4 black at $499.

The example illustrates how the start-up began with a simple first product aimed at the niche market of surfers. It then expanded product range and target audience. The aim was to offer customers more choice and keep the competition out.[6]

Less driven by excitement for new technology than innovators, pragmatists like to compare your new product and its pros and cons with different alternatives available on the market. So, winning over pragmatic early adopters and the early majority requires thinking about how to create competition. Simply identifying substitutes and explaining to customers your product's benefits over these alternatives may be sufficient. Offering product trials will help to reduce scepticism and persuade customers that your product, indeed, outperforms the competition. Leaving obvious comparisons out of the equation is bound to backfire and create customer distrust.

7.5 Price: how to set your price

Support for a sustainable business model

Price should reflect the value of your product. If the relationship is right, and if priced competitively compared with competing products, customers should be willing to engage in exchange. However, switching costs should be accounted for, including old accessories that do not fit the new product and need replacement, installation costs and the time required to train staff to learn how to use the new product. Particularly in the case of a radically new product, these costs may be substantial and even dominate the adoption decision of prospective customers. For instance, the Velotype – a machine that was introduced in 1983 in Amsterdam that relied on typing sets of letters rather than individual ones – never made inroads because it required retraining existing secretaries. The lack of word-processing standards also played a role in its lack of success. In 1991, the firm filed for bankruptcy. In 1998, the company got a second life, but sales remained difficult. In 2011, the Velotype PRO® keyboard was launched, an improved version that can be connected to all types of operating systems. It is successful in the niche market of professional subtitling (of television programmes). Allowing a skilled user to type at twice the speed of a skilled secretary, the keyboard is now specifically targeted at live applications, such as subtitling for television and real-time speech-to-text services.[7]

All too often, entrepreneurs claim that their product is unique and valuable. However, the proof of the value of a product lies in the market that will develop and in the price that customers are willing to pay. If a new product has value, customers are willing to engage in exchange and pay the price. If customers are unwilling to pay the price, the performance/price ratio of the new product should be seriously reconsidered. If high price is the main problem, this suggests that the business model that was developed for the start-up requires revisiting. If low product performance is the root cause, this issue should be resolved first; customers' minimum require-ments should be met first. Depending on the increase in performance, the price level can be established.

It is fair to say that pricing new products is a difficult task, probably more difficult than developing a promotion strategy or even finding a distributor. Pricing strategy must maintain a balance between covering the costs of development and production and achieving a reasonable profit while at the same time recognising the customers' price tolerance and value percep-tions.[8] Pricing is further complicated by the difficulty in predicting both the size of the potential market and the start-up's future market share. This introduces several unknown factors into the break-even analysis and into estimating the time required to break even. Rapid decline in price levels in technologically-driven markets is another important problem. Some companies have reported price declines of 20 per cent or more annually on technologies they have introduced.

In the next section, we will discuss the economic principles underlying price formation, and how the number of providers in the market and level of product differentiation, as well as free flow of market information, affect pricing decisions. The impact of scale and learning effects on production costs and price elasticity will also be discussed.

Example – Ludwick Marishane, targeting the bottom of the pyramid

In the small towns of Limpopo, South Africa, the water supply is as unpredictable as the weather. In his funny talk from TED@ Johannesburg (www.ted.com/talks/ludwick_marishane_a_bath_without_water.html; accessed 16 December 2016), young entrepreneur Ludwick Marishane tells his story of how he created 'DryBath', a cheap and convenient soap that does not require water. He developed the formula, performed market research and wrote his 40-page business plan all on his cell phone. He targets both poor people and rich kids, offering cleanness and convenience respectively.

Recognising that poor people do not buy products in bulk, he decided to package the product in innovative little sachets, easy to snap open and offering a single serving at five rand per sachet (equivalent to 0.46 dollars). Although slightly more expensive (i.e. higher $/volume price than large packages), it better caters to his target customers, particularly those at the bottom of the pyramid.

Economic roots

Economic theory asserts that in a free economy, the market price reflects interaction between supply and demand for a product. That is, the price is set so as to balance the quantity supplied and the quantity demanded. Sometimes, the price may be distorted by factors such as tax and other government regulations.

An important assumption of general economic theory is complete or perfect information. It refers to a situation in which knowledge about other market participants is available to all participants. This assumption leads to immediate adjustments to changes in price levels throughout the market.

The way demand and supply interact and the price that emerges is affected by market structure. *Market structure* refers to the number of firms producing identical products. At one extreme, we find perfect competition. Characterised by an unlimited number of producers and customers that sell and buy a homogeneous product, in theory, no one has market power and, as a result of perfect information, the price level will be driven down to the level of cost price. At the other extreme, we find monopoly: a market with only one provider of a product or service and many customers. In this case, the firm has a lot of market power and can dictate the price. When the firm decides on pricing, it will only take the chance of customers leaving the market or switching to substitutes, or endangering other firms entering into the market. In between these extremes, we find market structures such as oligopoly (a market dominated by a small number of firms that each has a major market share and thus market power) and monopolistic competition (a market where a large number of firms exist and each has a small market share as a result of slightly differentiated products).

This suggests that market structure, level of product homogeneity and the degree to which parties in the market have information all affect the price level in a market. The market structure is the backdrop against which prices are set. So, start-ups should carefully consider the number and nature of the competition they are up against when setting prices.

Two additional economic principles need to be explained. First, the impact of *learning and scale effects* on price. The assumption is that with increased volume, scale and learning effects occur, which will reduce production costs and, consequently, lower market prices. Learning and scale effects explain the rapid decline of price levels for many technologies after market introduction and increased success. For instance, although at introduction, digital cameras (LCD projectors, plasma TVs, etc.) were very expensive, today they are inexpensive. As more customers buy these products, manufacturers can produce on a larger scale, which drives down cost. This effect is fuelled by increased experience in production.

Second, one should understand price elasticity. *Price elasticity* refers to changes in customer demand in response to small changes in price levels. It is an important factor to include when considering prices and price strategies. Price elasticity is high if an increase of price by one unit (e.g. *x* euros) results in a significant change in demand (also one unit or more). Prices are inelastic if such an increase triggers no or only a small change in demand (e.g. with gasoline or petrol, but also many basic food products such as bread – people will not consume less when prices increase). If prices are inelastic, a firm will find it easier to recoup costs than when prices are elastic. Much depends on the availability of alternatives; the more alternatives, the more options customers have and thus the more elastic prices will be.

Pricing methods

We will discuss the three basic price-setting methods: *cost-based pricing*, *competitor-based pricing* and *customer- (or value-)based pricing*. The first approach focuses on calculating costs and then adding a profit margin, or return on investment mark-up. It is a basic, simple pricing method.

It requires estimating future sales volume, which is particularly difficult for new products. The approach does not consider market conditions such as competition and demand. High cost levels translate into high list prices, whereas low cost prices make low list prices.

The other two pricing methods do account, at least to some extent, for market conditions. *Competitor-based pricing* uses competitor prices as a point of reference. Either the market leader or closest alternative is used to set a price. A slightly higher or lower price will be chosen based on arguments of quality and reputation, or simply in an attempt to gain market share. *Customer-based pricing* relies mainly, but not exclusively, on customers' perceptions of the benefits of a product. It sets prices based primarily on the value to the customer, perceived or estimated. However, costs and competitive motivations are also often accounted for.

While the cost-based pricing method is commonly used to price commodities, customer-based pricing is most successful for products that have a demonstrably higher value, usually aimed at niche markets. This pricing method is also applied for products that are in short supply, or that are sold largely based on emotion.

Caterpillar, for example, is known for using value-based pricing of its construction and mining equipment, diesel and natural gas engines, industrial gas turbines and diesel-electric locomotives. Their sales agents begin by referring to the price of a similar piece of equipment from a competitor and then explain that the Caterpillar brand charges extra for greater reliability, durability and better quality of spare parts and service (e.g. $5,000, $4,000 and $1,000 respectively). If the competitor's tractor sells at, for instance, $90,000, they argue that the Caterpillar product is worth $100,000 and that their list price of $97,500 is, in fact, a good deal.[9]

Pricing strategies

The pricing strategy for a new product should be developed to achieve the desired impact on the market while discouraging competition; it should be closely intertwined with pricing itself. Two basic strategies to achieve this are *skimming pricing* and *penetration pricing*.

Skimming pricing aims to skim the cream off the market by using a relatively high initial price for a product or service, and then lowering it over time in order to reach more customers. The price is often based on some competitive advantage such as holding a patent with its limited time span, or having a first-mover advantage that will decline over time. It is recommended for conditions when the nature of demand is uncertain, when the competition requires some time to develop and market a similar product and when the product is so innovative that first customers are willing to pay the price. Due to the high price, market development will be slow. To tap the mass market the price will be lowered later. For a financially weak company, a skimming strategy may enable it to gain a strong position in a market and make a good profit while avoiding high investments in promotion and production levels to cultivate and meet demand.

However, this strategy has some drawbacks. Skimming can encourage competitors to enter the market. When other firms see the high margins, they may enter quickly. Furthermore, skimming results in a slow rate of adoption and diffusion and may ultimately jeopardise a start-up's first-mover advantage.

Penetration pricing is the strategy of entering the market with a low initial price to attract customers and capture a large market share as soon as possible. High price elasticity (i.e. demand sensitive to price difference) is probably the most important reason to adopt a penetration strategy. If demand is elastic (i.e. price sensitive) over the entire demand spectrum, penetration is preferred over skimming. Penetration pricing discourages competitors from entering the market. Low price implies low margins, which should defer competitor interest. However, one may also use the penetration strategy to develop the market at large. Anticipating serious market development and aiming for future economies of scale, the introduction price then can be set much lower than prototype cost levels in anticipation of serious cost reductions once sales volume increases (due to scale and learning effects). However, this approach works only when the new product caters to the needs of the mass market and it should be designed accordingly.

Thus, both competitors and the various responses to your market launch should play a significant role when thinking about price strategy. If your competitor is an established firm that is dependent on the market that you enter, you can be sure that it will put up a fight. An aggressive price decrease should be expected from them, which may reduce the chance for your new product to make inroads, particularly if its introduction price is set high. Scenarios and role plays anticipating this kind of competitor response and how your firm can react should be developed.

Doing the right thing – Anticipating competitive moves

You have spent lots of time, manpower and money developing your radically new innovative product. You are ready to bring it to the market. Do not let a lack of preparedness kill your business. Begin with anticipating possible competitor responses and how your firm may react 'in the case of'. As well as being a lot of fun, it is an excellent exercise in developing contingency plans (i.e. scenarios for responding to all the surprise moves that can happen and the possible effects these may have on your business). This type of preparation is particularly relevant to your pricing strategy, as you cannot change it easily once you have begun implementing it.

Price components and structure

Many factors make up the components of price, including (1) development costs, (2) production costs, (3) marketing and sales costs, (4) distribution costs and (5) the margin required or desired. However, (6) discounts (types of discount that will be used) and (7) service/warranty costs should also be taken into account. Forgetting some of these cost factors will hurt margins significantly because price levels are often difficult to increase once they have been established.

In calculating the price that the customer pays, it is important to consider their *total cost of ownership of the product*. This refers to the purchase price plus cost of operations. It includes, for example, installation, costs for operating the product (including service costs, years of operation, use of raw materials), training of staff, possible changes to their logistics, IT and so on. If the total cost of ownership is reduced, this is beneficial to the customer and thus vitally important information to use when setting and explaining the price to the customer. However, a customer will only switch if the decision maker believes the claims and is sensitive to the issue raised. As long as customers stay with their old beliefs, no progress will be made and scepticism will remain. Also, when the decision maker does not benefit from the long-term cost benefits, no progress will be made. For example, LED lights have a much higher life expectancy than traditional lamps or energy-saving SL lamps. Manufacturers use this to justify a high price for their new LED lamps in an attempt to prevent price erosion. However, as suppliers used similar claims for previous innovations (e.g. halogen headlights for cars) and these have proved largely false, customers were sceptical, unwilling to be burned a second time.

In arriving at a suitable price, the mark-ups along the value chain must be factored in too. It is one thing to cover product costs, but the costs and margins added by distributors ultimately determine the final price that customers have to pay. If that final price is beyond the customers' tolerance level, the start-up must re-evaluate all costs and margins and may have to make some radical changes. The start-up may have to resort to direct channels to avoid these mark-ups.

Finally, entrepreneurs should be careful when offering discounts early on in the process of gaining customer interest.[10] Faced with pressure to make early sales and generate cash flow, many start-ups tend to offer serious price discounts in order to close initial deals. It may, however, establish unsustainable pricing precedents, particularly if the news of the discounts spreads around the industry. Therefore, it is advisable to maintain list prices and use alternative ways to increase the value for prospects, such as offering free shipping, a free trial period or a discount on orders placed before a certain date.

7.6 Promotion: creating awareness with a limited budget

The communication process and promotion mix

Entrepreneurs face a tremendous challenge: they need to create awareness in the market for their *reputationless* new product application and company. *Awareness* refers to the level and accessibility of the knowledge customers have about your products and firm; the higher the level and accessibility of this knowledge, the higher the level of awareness. *Positive association* concerns positive thoughts related to particular features or attributes of a product, brand or organisation.

Customer awareness and positive associations are created using promotional activities. However, before we can continue we first should explain the communication process and promotion instruments available to a start-up.

Communication

Communication refers to a process of transfer of information between two parties. It typically involves a sender, a message and a recipient. Communication requires that the communicating parties share an area of communication commonality. For a start-up and its prospective customers, this is the market or business context. A communication process is complete once the receiver has understood the message of the sender.

Personal and impersonal communications can be distinguished as follows. Impersonal communication refers to mass communication that is aired broadly. In this case, the sender has little control over the communication process and limited chances to make sure the sender actually receives the message. In contrast, personal communication is direct and generally allows for feedback from the receiver, which can help establish that the message was received and interpreted correctly.

Another frequently made distinction is between verbal and non-verbal communications. The former involves language, whereas the latter refers to the fact that firm and salesperson behaviour, product features, packaging and even price, among others, tend to also communicate. For instance, high price may signal quality. Such non-verbal communication may be intended or unintended, yet always holds important cues for customers.

The ultimate goal of a start-up's business communications is to sell its new product. However, to do this, the start-up must first attract attention. But drawing attention is only a secondary goal. The start-up's message or announcement should also contain matter that will interest and persuade after the attention has been obtained.

Based on these principles, advertisers have developed a persuasion model labelled AIDA: attention, interest, desire and action (see Figure 7.1). AIDA describes a common list of events that may occur sequentially when a consumer engages with communication, such as an advertisement or meeting with a salesperson. *Attention* refers to the need to attract the attention of the prospective customer and thus for creating awareness. *Interest* involves raising customer interest by focusing on and demonstrating product advantages and benefits instead of focusing on features, as is often the case in traditional advertising of many high-tech products. *Desire* concerns persuading customers that they want and desire the new product or service and that it will satisfy their needs. Finally, *action* is persuading lead customers towards taking action, and thus, to try and buy the new product.

Using a model like this gives the entrepreneur a framework for approaching a market effectively using communications. Moving from left to right, one moves closer to the positive attitude of the prospect for the

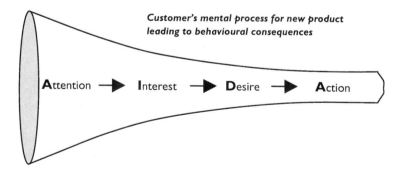

Figure 7.1 AIDA communication model

new product and the customer's action to buy. In this 'funnel', some percentage of prospects will be lost. By monitoring the process and the percentages of customers lost at each stage, a start-up can identify and then remedy bottlenecks with its marketing actions.

Promotion mix

In deciding how best to promote their new product, start-ups must decide which promotional instruments to use. These decisions must consider the start-up's objectives, as well as the merits of and costs entailed in using different promotional instruments. Some instruments can reach some customer groups better than others; some are very focused and personal, while others transmit broadly and impersonally. The promotion mix includes advertising, personal selling, sales promotion, public relations and social media.

- *Advertising.* This concerns any paid form of non-personal presentation and promotion of a new product or idea by an identified source or sponsor. It includes media such as print ads, radio and television, but also brochures and catalogues, direct mail and websites.
- *Personal selling.* This involves person-to-person presentation of a new product or idea aimed at introducing one or more prospects to or stimulating them to buy your new product or service. It includes, for instance, sales presentations, telemarketing and incentive programmes for intermediaries.
- *Sales promotion.* Incentives designed to stimulate the purchase or sale of a product. It entails, for example, product samples, rebates, trade shows and demonstrations involving reference customers.
- *Public relations.* This is essentially free advertising or word of mouth. It varies from newspaper and magazine coverage, to television and radio presentations, to positive references in speeches.
- *Social media.* This refers to exposure and positive referral in the entrepreneur's social network via, for instance, LinkedIn (business oriented), Facebook, Myspace (personal dimension), blogs (e.g. Blogger), YouTube (a website for sharing videos) and Twitter. Because these networks are voluntary and social, the communications and information provided should not be obtrusive.

Together, these promotion instruments make up the *promotion mix*. As the word 'mix' suggests, the instruments should be integrated for a maximum effect. It suggests that a common theme should be used for maximum effect and efforts should complement one another over time.

Some instruments are more useful for creating awareness (e.g. advertising, PR and social media), whereas others are better for informing prospective customers in detail (e.g. technical brochure, personal selling and demonstration). Yet other instruments can help create action and thus stimulate a customer to move towards purchasing (e.g. a discount or offering something extra such as a year of free maintenance or service).

During the customer discovery and validation stages, more personal approaches may be useful, particularly those allowing for two-way interaction. Once the target market and product configuration have been established, more mass-marketing options might be considered.

The challenge of establishing brand presence

A strong brand presence is a significant competitive advantage in markets where customers have many choices. A *brand* refers to the personality that identifies a product, service or company and generally includes a brand name and a sign or symbol, or combination thereof. The psychological aspect is sometimes referred to as the brand image. It is a symbolic construct created within the minds of people, consisting of all the information and expectations associated with the brand and its product.

A brand acts as a point of recognition and affinity, two things start-ups typically lack. So, it rather applies to the customer creation and company building stages.

To build brand recognition and affinity with prospective customers, a start-up should follow the AIDA model mentioned. The first hurdle is creating awareness. Awareness will pave the way for creating brand associations and attitudes. Associations refer to evaluations of certain cognitions or beliefs about a brand. Positive associations generate positive emotions and affect. Negative associations lead to dislike. By fostering the positive and preventing negative associations, a positive overall attitude is stimulated, which is known to be the driver of preference and buying intention. Therefore, the aim is to create a positive brand attitude and image.

Example – Tesla: building positive brand associations

At the start, electrical cars were not associated with speed and endurance. Battery life was one of the problems. To create positive associations of electrical driving and the Tesla brand in particular, the firm placed its electrical engine and batteries in a Lotus Elise sports car. They then organised a roadshow to engage the public and give everyone the opportunity to see and experience the roadster. Although the car was extremely expensive to purchase, it helped demonstrate that electrical power and speedy cars are a happy marriage, creating positive brand associations.

The positive associations a start-up wants can be derived from the *unique selling points* (USPs) of its technology and application. Once these USPs have been validated with early customers, they can act as a 'reason to believe' in its communication message to subsequent prospects. Providing evidence that the new product application and technology will deliver as promised, and have a higher value than the alternative of the competition, will help to build a convincing brand image.

There are several *branding strategies*. These vary from a similar firm-product name, called corporate branding (e.g. GE, Shell), to using separate names for the firm and new product, called individual branding (e.g. Procter and Gamble's product Pampers). Hybrid forms are also possible (e.g. Apple's iPod, Mac, iTunes). The single name approach reduces communication costs but allows for little differentiation between products or product lines. Moreover, it makes the organisation vulnerable as reputation damage affects everything the company produces. The use of separate names offers flexibility but is costly and prevents synergy. The hybrid solution offers the best of both worlds.

Carefully considering the *brand architecture* that fits your situation best and selecting a name that resonates with your prospective customers and that also triggers the right associations is important. For instance, if you plan to expand abroad, make sure your brand name can travel. Pre-testing the name with customers can prevent a lot of trouble and unnecessary costs. An example is Dutch start-up Inmotio. The name refers to the nature of the product, which tracks and traces athletes during a game. Further, the firm uses the English translation to make the name easier to transfer internationally. Face validity supported it and some basic tests were used to validate it.

Useful promotion and social media strategies for start-ups

Promotion budgets can be fixed, they can be a percentage of turnover or they can be set with a particular communication goal in mind. Start-ups, however, often have limited resources and small promotion budgets.

Only by being extremely creative can maximum promotional effect be accomplished. Here are some suggestions.

1 *Take advantage of publicity.* For a start-up, any cheap opportunity to promote its new product is welcome. So actively planning for and stimulating free publicity is important. If a start-up's new product, goal or mission is newsworthy, entrepreneurs can obtain publicity by contacting a newspaper, magazine or online report to share their story. To take advantage of free publicity, start-ups need to develop a press kit that includes background articles on the firm, press releases, ideas for stories and sample articles that have already been written. Evidence of the effectiveness of the new product will also be welcome. This will increase the news organisation's interest.

Example – Free publicity

PreventionCompass, a start-up, benefited substantially from coverage in *The Economist.*[11] The article appeared in its 'Science and Technology' section. The message was that prevention is an important way to reduce increases in healthcare costs. Here are two excerpts from the article, which clearly show the excellent PR the start-up received:

[T]here may be a solution in the form of a personalized health check-up called PreventionCompass. This system has been developed by the Institute for Prevention and Early Diagnostics (NIPED), a firm based in Amsterdam. It requires the customer to answer a detailed questionnaire about his way of life and to undergo a series of tests. It draws its conclusions [regarding risk factors for certain diseases e.g. cancer, cardiovascular disease, diabetes and kidney disease] by running the results through a 'knowledge system' – a database that pools expertise from many sources.

This year two large insurance companies, which provide corporate healthcare, income and disability insurance to employees are offering to lower the premiums of customers who sign up to PreventionCompass. Next year the plan is to extend the scheme more widely, by recruiting Dutch GPs [general practitioners] to offer it to people from lower income groups who do not have such private health insurance. The message, then, is

> prevention, not cure. And it is a message that needs to be heeded across the world as poor countries grow wealthier and adopt the eating habits and sedentary lives of the rich.[12]

2   *Use the power of the Internet.* The Internet has opened up completely new, exciting ways to generate free publicity. Buzz or viral marketing refers to any marketing technique that induces websites or users to pass on a marketing message to other sites or users, creating a potentially exponential growth in the message's visibility and effect. It requires interaction between customers (and users) of a product or service to amplify the original marketing message. Positive buzz and potential goodwill for your new product, start-up or cause are the objective. Buzz marketing works because prospective customers trust individuals more than organisations that have vested interests in promoting their products and/or services.

Today, social media is a vital channel for marketing communication. The impact depends on the influence the entrepreneur has in his or her established small network and the quality and size of this network. Not the first-tier but the second- and third-tier contacts are what matters – so the contacts of your contacts and beyond. This represents the potential *multiplier effect* that your message will receive.

Chat rooms and blogs are also popular media for electronic marketing campaigns. As an entrepreneur seeking to draw attention, it is important to seek out the authors with the right blogs to influence and create the right buzz. The closer the match between the blog's readership and the product, the higher the impact. The nature of a blog guarantees the continuous attention of the target audience. Consistent with this, the entrepreneur or customer-building team should also participate continuously in the blog or in discussions of related topics in chat rooms.

Several suggestions can be made to gain the maximum impact for your marketing efforts on the Internet (and social media) and to prevent basic mistakes:[13]

- *Keep your message simple.* Simple messages spread across social networks more easily.
- *Say what is new.* A message must be relevant and newsworthy for people for them to forward it to others, so make it exciting – even theatrical – but accurate.
- *Do not make claims you cannot support.* Making false claims will kill buzz or, worse, will lead to negative buzz.

- *Refrain from directly advertising your brand or firm.* Clear advertisements will be seen as a breach of trust and will trigger negative responses. Social media is not commercial television!
- *Ensure continuity.* Social media thrives on continued exchange of information. Continuous and courteous messages and responses are very important. It requires a mind shift; rather than fitting everything in one message, the trick is to use different issues and points of view to create new content. This will help to interest your audience and create followers.

Finally, carefully watch the communities that are already successful with marketing online and learn from their activities and achievements. To proceed with your marketing efforts, pay attention to other start-ups' methods. Use what works, but avoid their mistakes.

Doing it right – Internet as promotion and business model option

The Internet can be used to draw attention to your start-up and create awareness for your new product, but it can also be used for *crowd funding*. Very often, young entrepreneurs use online marketing to leverage their network of friends. The following example shows an email that I received from a start-up that illustrates the idea well:

Dear Ed,

We would like to let you know about our start-up. We are really excited and passionate about it. But, we will need your support!

Driven by our passion for quality healthy food, our love of exploring new tastes and our will to support small artisan producers that insist on quality, we founded Maryo Artisan Products. We aim to make Maryo a company that will form the single link between artisan producers of Greece and end-consumers in Europe. Our first product is a unique, very low acidity Extra Virgin Olive Oil produced in Agarathos monastery in Crete. Our idea was to take a top quality olive oil that until now was found only in perfume size super-expensive bottles and make it an every-day healthy habit. This is our idea in a nutshell!

But we need some support. As we all know, the first people that will trust a new company and try their products are those that have some connection with the founders and thus some

> trust. This is why we turn to our friends, our professors, our colleagues . . .
>
> So, join our journey, support us by placing your order in our crowd funding page: http://igg.me/at/maryo-artisan-products
>
> . . . Another great way to help us will be to share our story within your circle!
>
> Thank you so much!

3   *Use trade fairs.* Participating in or visiting trade fairs is a good way to expand your network and increase the chances of finding prospects. Trade fairs attract people who are interested in a particular topic and allow for face-to-face contact. Trade fair visitors also tend to be more curious and innovative. Therefore, fairs are the ideal situation for customer discovery. Because fairs offer the opportunity of personal contact and interaction, you are in an excellent position to explain your product and get feedback. So, trade fairs also help make a first or second step towards customer validation.

4   *Use pre-announcement.*[14] Pre-announcement is a tactic particularly to promote new products using new technology. It makes prospective customers aware of the new development and can potentially persuade them to delay their purchasing a product until the new application is ready. Although generally used by established firms, it also is a useful approach for start-ups. Through pre-announcement, a start-up can create a market position until the product actually reaches the market.

However, pre-announcement only makes sense if the start-up can also deliver. In this case, it can help create customer awareness for the new product and educate the market.

There are also potential negative effects of pre-announcement. Not only will prospective customers be alerted to the new product, but so will the competition, offering them extra time to get prepared and react. Therefore, to protect the pioneering advantage many start-ups do not pre-announce. The decision is, however, best made based on actual competitive advantage and need for the market to be educated about the new technology. Finally, informal buzz is probably safer and more powerful than formal pre-announcement.

Create dissatisfaction

Although innovative customers may be actively searching for new and better solutions, customers typically need a trigger and certain level of

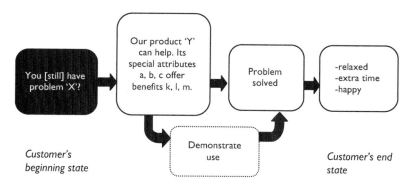

Figure 7.2 Customer dissatisfaction and advertising the benefits of the new product

dissatisfaction to switch providers. Dissatisfied customers are motivated to search and thus are open to new alternatives. Satisfied customers will generally not be interested unless the entrepreneur can create a new ideal situation and a desire in these customers to attain this new ideal.

This is why many communications we see around us appeal to a particular problem and some kind of user frustration. The message is that the problem shown can be solved using the brand of the start-up. In the process, particular product features are highlighted and the unique benefits offered are mentioned. It facilitates prospective customers to recognise the problem and frustrations involved, and to also understand how the new product works and is linked to (latent) needs. By presenting the new product in the right use context, the communication builds customer knowledge and association. The communication approach is illustrated in Figure 7.2. Drawing on means-end psychological principles, this approach has been proven to be very powerful.

7.7 Place: obtaining market access

Gaining access to customers

Place refers to distribution, and therefore all the available options to deliver the new product to your target audience. It involves three decisions: (1) where customers should be able to buy the product (channel decisions); (2) how to ship it to the customer (physical distribution); and (3) how to manage the relationships with distributors (trade marketing).

Short and long *channels of distribution* can be distinguished. In the case of short channels, no intermediate partners exist between a firm and its customer, while in a long channel, multiple stages exist – for instance, between wholesale and retail, there are several intermediaries. Although the trend is to reduce the number of layers of distribution and rely more on direct channels, most markets still use some form of intermediaries. This decision is often motivated by another issue. Often, firms do not just rely on a single channel but use multiple channels to reach customers. They offer customers a choice of how and where to obtain the product, and thus offer convenience. Certain channels may align better with the needs of particular customer groups.

Sometimes, complex products require special assistance or installation (e.g. an element in a production system such as a labelling machine). Having high-quality distributors or so-called *value-added resellers* is required and a key success factor for your business. If your product really benefits from careful advice and implementation assistance, it is important to find good and, most of all, reliable partners. Apart from the most obvious partners, you may also consider partners that service the same customers but sell complementary rather than substitute products. For instance, a small student-driven start-up, Senz (www.senz.com/en/collections/lookbook-globetrotter/; accessed 16 December 2016), which had invented a new storm umbrella, teamed up with Mexx clothing stores rather than luggage stores to penetrate the European market. At the start, the umbrella was offered in the 50 largest Mexx stores. Within nine days, stocks were sold out. Another option is to look for a large competitor and ride piggyback. It will only work if your products offer something extra over the competitor's current product line.

The Internet is a popular way for start-ups to gain distribution access. The Internet is a low-cost option because no expensive presentation and showroom are needed, and shipping only occurs when an order and payment have been received. It is a particularly attractive option if access to distribution is difficult to obtain due to a dominant competitor controlling the (alternative) channel(s). The Internet option may also be combined with, for instance, operating a direct sales force that directly approaches customers. Integrating the two options can help to accomplish synergy.

Motivations of distributors to carry the start-up's brand

Just like customers, distributors buy for a reason. They have their own reasons to add your product to their product line and to want to represent your start-up. It is good to keep this in mind when approaching them. Motivations for distributors include:

1 *Customers ask for the product.* If the new product offers clear benefits that address latent needs, and if customers are aware of the product and start-up's existence, they may approach distributors. In the case of a start-up, serious pull marketing (e.g. via the Internet or free publicity) must have been developed to create such demand pull. However, distributors may also anticipate such a development and proactively adopt the new product. If the product strategy of the start-up and distributor are aligned, this may be the case. It may bring extra customers and help to better satisfy existing customers.

2 *More favourable margin.* If your product offers much the same value as previous products but offers a much better margin, this may also persuade the distributor to switch.

3 *An opportunity to reduce the current product range.* If, by stocking your product, the distributor can prune its product line, the product is attractive to stock. For instance, if you offer a new industrial or professional glue or kit that can be used under wet and dry conditions and can stand temperatures over 100 degrees Celsius, the distributor needs to carry fewer items to satisfy the same demand and can use remaining shelf space to sell other products.

4 *Enhanced positioning.* Some products and brands offer a distributor the chance to enhance its positioning. For instance, if adoption of the start-up's product helps a distributor to enhance its image of quality or product leadership, this may be an important motivation for the distributor to decide in favour of the start-up's new product and to adopt and carry it. For example, if your start-up has developed a better type of solar cell or coloured, designer-like photovoltaic (PV) panels to place on the facade of buildings, any distributor working at the high end of the market may be interested, as it will help enhance their positioning.

By understanding the motivations of distributors, a start-up can better prepare its sales pitch and negotiate a deal.

The quality of distribution

For any start-up, obtaining access to customers in the market is important. The best channels are probably those that your target customers are using most frequently. However, these may be blocked by competitors. Consequently, you may have to look elsewhere. By aligning your strategy with the available channel, you may be able to create access and a niche position.

Generally, more and less important distribution channels can be distinguished. Analysing product flows by channel can offer important insight into which channel is important for which product and to reach which customer group. However, not only the static numbers but also changes that are taking place are important. For instance, in retail it used to be said that only one thing mattered: location, location, location. Yet, over the past few years, a significant shift towards buying on the Internet has occurred, suggesting that this important retail law no longer applies.

Considering alternative channels is also important. While supermarkets are struggling to keep customers interested, and are exploring Internet sales, some new ventures have adopted and developed alternative channels. Today, customers like convenience and fresh products. As a result, we have seen a surge in vending machines selling fresh products in many countries, and pickup points have grown in many markets as an alternative form of distribution.

Some important indicators of distribution quality you can consider are (1) market coverage; (2) the selection indicator; and (3) share in turnover in the product category (of your product). Market coverage refers to how many distributors carry your brand compared with all distributors selling products from this category. The selection indicator shows whether your brand is presented by larger or smaller distributers; it compares the turnover for your distributors in this product category with the average turnover of all active distributors (selection indicator = 1 means average, whereas a score of larger or smaller than 1 refers to presence in larger and smaller than average stores respectively). Finally, share in turnover reflects the part of turnover your brand has in your distributors' total sales in this category. It refers to the market share you have with your distributors.

Using such detailed analysis will help monitor and evaluate your start-up's current distribution situation and build additional distribution presence.

Doing the right thing – Avoid channel conflict

Although a start-up's main concern will be to obtain distribution and rapid sales, the search for distribution access and cooperation may result in operating different channels simultaneously. As a result, channel conflicts may emerge. Channel conflict is, for example, when you have attracted a distributor but you are also selling to customers directly. It is important to develop guidelines concerning how to divide the market to clarify which customers are approached and served by whom and how. You should also clarify how to act when customers get mixed up between the different channels – who should serve and profit?

The danger of exclusive distribution

Distributors may ask for an exclusive deal. This may seem a good idea, particularly if the distributor has exactly the type of customers you are looking for. However, it is important to understand the potential danger involved. Sometimes, this request can be a strategic move from the distributor aimed at protecting its existing business and business relations. By signing an exclusive deal, the start-up limits its strategic options and puts its faith in the hands of the partner. The partner can then make or break the start-up. If the partner minimises rather than maximises the efforts for pushing the start-up's products, legal action may be required but that is difficult. Although the start-up may try to get out of the contract, its limited size, resources and time may prove a serious barrier to setting things right. As a result, the start-up may have no other option, but to look elsewhere for developing its business.

Thus, start-ups should be careful when signing exclusive deals. Often, joining forces not with the establishment but rather with a new channel or with a channel that is under pressure may prove more promising.

Next to the option of exclusive distribution, both *selective* and *intensive distribution strategies* exist. While exclusive distribution aims for a special, high-quality presentation of a product, selective distribution relies on a confined set of distributors to present a brand. It is a common format, for instance, in installation services and in selling computer software. These distributors have been selected and certified to guarantee their quality. A third option is intensive distribution. In this case, the start-up aims to achieve broad market presence and makes its product or service widely available to all customers when and where they want it. In particular, convenience products are distributed in this way. Providers of capital goods generally rely on the other two options.

Summary

- A simple plan can help guide marketing and sales efforts. The plan can be updated and improved over time in response to opportunities.

- The content of the plan will depend on the stage of the customer development process. It should be developed and managed by the customer development team, who should be accountable.
- The plan should focus on building customer value, market presence and customer relationships. First, assumptions about customer value, market and target customers should be validated. Second, a consistent programme should be developed that can be rolled out to the market at large later.
- Marketing activities include the four Ps: product, price, promotion and place. The first two are closely related to creating customer value. The latter two are for building market presence.
- Creativity, cooperating with partners and using the latest online marketing options can help obtain maximum marketing exposure at minimum expense.

Notes

1 Allen (2010).
2 See, for example, DiBenedetto (1999). The three components are comparable to the three elements of customer equity used by Rust *et al.* (2000).
3 Webb *et al.* (2011).
4 Lafley (2004: 51).
5 See, for example, Srinivasan *et al.* (2012).
6 See www.yahoo.com/news/gopro-history-success-230730979.html?ref=gs (accessed 16 December 2016) and en.wikipedia.org/wiki/GoPro#HERO_ cameras (accessed 16 December 2016).
7 See www.velotype.com/en/ (accessed 16 December 2016).
8 Allen (2010).
9 Mullins *et al.* (2005).
10 Fogel *et al.* (2012).
11 *The Economist* (2007).
12 For more information, see www.vitalinnovators.nl (accessed 16 December 2016).
13 Rosen (2002).
14 Allen (2010).

Chapter 8

The role of sales in customer development

Key issues

- Explain the principle of the sales learning curve.
- Understand the knowledge brokering function of sales and the importance of connecting sales to the team of engineers developing the new product.
- Present the sales process and its relationship with customer development.
- Discuss the development of a sales message to successfully hunt for prospects.
- Stress the importance of managing customer expectations.

8.1 The sales learning curve

In Chapter 7, we introduced the one-page marketing and sales plan. We explained that the plan should guide the start-up's customer development process and detail marketing goals and actions. It should be developed and managed by the customer development team.

One of the three core dimensions of the plan is developing customer relationships. It is a true new business development task and will require a major sales effort.

> What is needed ... are entrepreneurial sales skills; the ability to change presentations, customers and products on a daily basis, the ability to calmly process the news that the product features, schedules and functions have changed yet again. The ability to listen to customer objections and understand whether they are issues about the product,

the presentation, the pricing, or something else. There is no fixed price list and product presentation that will last more than a week. What we need early on in sales is an individual comfortable with chaos and uncertainty who can close an order and not worry about building an organization. The goal of our first salesperson is to validate the business model by developing a sales roadmap, closing orders, and doing this without having a real product in hand. This may or may not be someone who can manage and build a sales department later.[1]

This early selling involves serious learning, which unfolds through the experimentation with different market segments and prototypes. It involves a give-and-take between the person in charge and the previously identified venturesome customers. Based on valuable customer feedback, as well as discussions and decisions undertaken by the customer development team, the organisation will modify its products. In addition, the processes for making and selling the product should be validated, discussed and improved. It will help to shape the start-up's message in describing the unique differences of the new product to potential customers.

This process of customer development takes time and a shortcut cannot be created simply by hiring more marketing staff or sending out more salespeople. Many problems are discovered sequentially, revealing themselves only after some preceding issue has been discovered and addressed. It involves a learning curve.[2]

If the person responsible for selling cannot find enough paying customers during the customer validation stage, the company needs to return to the drawing board. A new customer segment and its problems then should be identified in order to rediscover what customers want and will pay for. Validation acts as a checkpoint; until the start-up has validated its business model by finding (more) paying customers, marketing expenditures and size of the sales force – like all costs – should remain low. The moment that sales accelerate is the time to expand and build a sales force. Until that time, everything has to remain lean.

From a broader perspective, this entrepreneurial selling involves new business development and customer relationship development. The aim is to discover who the customer is and to develop the relationship with these customers. From a first sale, you want to move to repeat sales and maintaining or even extending the relationship. The aim is to move from a few initial customers to a portfolio of customers; from a small still fragile set to a broader, more stable and sustainable customer base. We continue with a discussion of the role of sales in our high-tech entrepreneurial setting, before discussing specific activities of sales that can help shape the third part of our one-page marketing and sales plan: the start-up's customer relationship development.

8.2 Sales as knowledge broker for innovation

Salespeople hold an important brokering role. Understanding this role helps to understand the challenges involved in the customer validation and creation stages.

As a liaison between outside customers and trends in the environment on the one hand, and colleagues inside the firm on the other hand, salespeople can connect and recombine knowledge about, for instance, the new product's development process with knowledge about customer product experiences they hear in the marketplace.[3] Salespeople who are aware of this important role will be able to contribute to their firm's short- and long-term goals (e.g. selling new products and establishing a strong market position). The more a salesperson connects with a multitude of colleagues internally and explores the information he or she has collected from outside, the richer the ideas and scenarios that will be developed which, if shared internally, will benefit the firm's capacity to effectively adapt its product application.

External customers can help salespeople understand the market, conceptualise customer problems that are the basis for new products and then better market these new products. Effectively transferring information from the external environment (e.g. customers) to the firm (e.g. new product developers) is important for generating ideas around new product development as well as for mustering internal support for altering the existing product concept. By involving venturous customers and salespeople in the new product development process, this knowledge transfer is stimulated.

Apart from these important inward- and outward-bound roles, salespeople also need to sell – to allocate attention and time to persuading customers to buy the start-up's new product. This will be difficult as long as the product validation has not yet succeeded and the new product's quality remains under par. Nevertheless, achieving actual sales for this product will be important to sustain a certain level of cash flow for the organisation. Therefore, it is key that salespeople are continuously motivated and get all possible support from their colleagues, including the entrepreneur him- or herself. Sales are a start-up's lifeline, next to venture capitalist confidence and support.

Salespeople with particular personal characteristics may be better knowledge brokers than others. Self-regulation literature[4] has identified two regulatory orientations as drivers of people's motivational capacity to guide themselves effectively towards important goals: the orientations of locomotion and assessment.

> Locomotion denotes movement away from a current state . . . , while assessment refers to evaluations of current states, goals, and means and comparisons among them. . . . [P]eople . . . differ in their preferences for locomotion and assessment, which influences the manner in which they approach tasks, pursue goals, make decisions, evaluate themselves and others, and deal with challenges.[5]

Together, locomotion and assessment encourage the extent to which a person is inclined to extract knowledge from external and internal sources. Salespeople who collect more knowledge and then integrate it with prior knowledge will be better knowledge brokers. Salespeople with technical and commercial knowledge will be best able to integrate both types of information involved. They can navigate effectively between the customers' needs and problems and new product development staffs' (technical) perspectives.

Connecting and integrating the salesperson(s) of your start-up with the organisation's engineering team is critical. It refers to the intensity with which the market insights generated by sales are accounted for in the start-up's internal new product development processes, and adds to the success of the firm's new product in the marketplace through two mechanisms (see Figure 8.1).[6] We will discuss this in more detail in the following section.

First, by relying on the knowledge of the salesperson about customer needs and feedback, the team of engineers will be able to pack more added value in the start-up's innovation, which will enhance its level of competitive advantage in the marketplace. Second, high sales integration with the engineering team will create emotional involvement and commitment of the salesperson for selling the new product. The salesperson will develop a positive attitude towards the new product, adopt it more confidently and, as a result, will be more motivated and work harder to persuade venturous customers to try and purchase it. Both these mechanisms increase the chance of the new product being accepted by the market and becoming a success.

Several factors moderate these two mechanisms and are potential levers for the customer development team to ensure an excellent involvement of the start-up's salesperson in the development of the start-up's innovation.

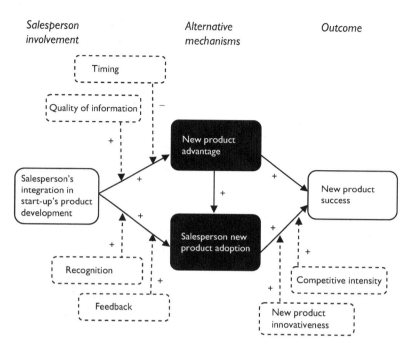

Figure 8.1 Connecting the start-up's sales and team of engineers (adapted from Kuester *et al.* 2016)

First, the relationship between salesperson integration and new product advantage is contingent on the quality of the knowledge transferred by the salesperson. If the market insights provided are valuable and directly useful for the development of the start-up's innovation by the team of engineers, the effect of salesperson integration on the innovation's product advantage will be increased. The same is true for early versus late involvement of sales in the process. Studies show that many important design decisions are made early in the engineering process. If these decisions are solely made by engineering, customer and market requirements, then trends are often not well accounted for. This impairs the success of many new products. Consistent with this, early sales involvement has been found to be worthwhile; it prevents mistakes and thus seriously enhances the relationship between salesperson integrations and the level of product advantage achieved. Finally, recognition of the salesperson by the engineering team and the level of feedback to the salesperson on how information was used to improve the new product's design also plays a role. High recognition creates sales' commitment, and thus positively moderates the path between integration and adoption of the new product by sales. Excellent feedback by the engineering team has a similar positive effect.

The level of success of the innovation in the marketplace depends on the level of product value or advantage of the new product and on the adoption of the new product by the salesperson(s). The relationship between salesperson adoption of the new product and success is contingent on the level of innovativeness of the new product and the competitive situation. Research has demonstrated that the successful management and reduction of uncertainties through communication and customer education are more important for radical new products. It also has shown that customer resistance to new product adoption is likely to increase for markets characterised by high levels of competitive intensity. Higher resistance emerges from customers' options to choose from a wider range of competing product offerings in markets where many suppliers are working hard to attract customers. Under these conditions, the impact of sales adoption on new product success will be higher; only if sales are well-motivated, creative and work hard to interest customers will progress in customer relationship development be made and the new product be successful.

The start-up's customer development team should be aware of (1) the importance of connecting the salesperson or staff to the organisation's engineering team and (2) the mechanisms through which this integration affects the success of the innovation in the marketplace. Specifically, the customer development team should stimulate sales to be connected and facilitate the knowledge brokering activities, as well as the diffusion and use of the information created. Timely involvement, mutual trust (recognition) and feedback loops need to be ensured and monitored.

8.3 Sales process and activities: developing customer relationships

Existing sales models are generally focused on established firms. They almost always assume that the salesperson has a fully developed product and clear price list, as well as a simple goal: to sell this product. The fact that initial sales activities are more focused on finding lead customers, listening to them to obtain feedback on the product concept and persuading them to help develop the new product is seldom addressed. However, not until the point where the new product and target customers are fixed, and

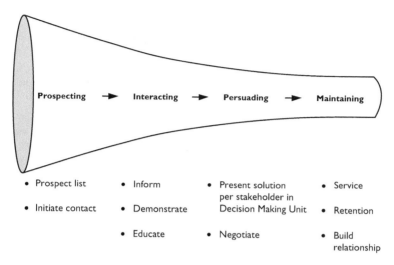

Figure 8.2 The selling process as a funnel

the sales roadmap is validated, can a switch to regular selling activities and approaches be implemented.

Regular selling involves four major stages: prospecting, interacting, persuading and maintaining the relationship. These are shown in Figure 8.2 together with several key activities.

Prospecting refers to the need for sales to develop a list of potential customers from the target segment. Marketing should provide help developing such a list. Together, marketing and sales can review prospective customers and identify the most promising ones for maximum effect. The next stage involves making initial contact. Because this is easier with a contact person on the other side (in the customer organisation), networking is important. Through one's own network, the name of a contact person can often be identified and an introduction made. The main objective is getting a first appointment. During the visit, the salesperson needs to listen carefully to obtain as much information from the prospect and his or her situation as possible. What are the problems at hand that need to be resolved? How does the start-up's product fit in? Another objective is informing the prospect about the start-up, its innovation and its services. A demonstration may help explain what the product can do, but this should be carefully planned to make sure the product functions well. A failure during a demonstration may have detrimental effects. Sometimes, some knowledge transfer or customer education may be desirable, or even necessary, to help the customer understand and appreciate the innovation, but also to gain maximum effect from a demonstration or trial.

As mentioned earlier, information collection is a very important sales task. By asking the right questions and listening carefully, information about reasons for and barriers to adoption can be discovered. Much can also be learned about who is involved in the decision and what they think is important. The data collection should involve finding out more about the *decision-making unit* (DMU) and different members' buying criteria.

The third stage is persuasion. If the customer is interested and the start-up can make a sales pitch, it is important to prepare well. This involves developing solutions for all stakeholders to maximise the chance of adoption. A negotiation strategy should also be developed in which a deal is outlined and the ultimate boundaries (e.g. lowest price) determined.

Finally, the product delivery and service stage is reached, which extends to the maintaining and extension of the relationship. The first stage, product delivery, is important to ensure a satisfied customer. The second, maintaining and extending the relationship, is helpful to grow the start-up's business.

Answering the following questions should help to develop the sales approach and the sales process:[7]

- *Prospecting.* Who are the prospects? Which prospects will you visit over the next six months? How will you reach and approach them? Who will you meet and what are their specific functions in their companies? How will you engage them in conversation?
- *Customer purchasing cycle and pipeline.* What are the key elements of the customer purchasing cycle and how will we lead prospects through this process? How, if necessary, will we modify our approach? How successful were we at each stage of the cycle and where are potential bottlenecks? Which customers are currently in the process and where? Which specific obstacles exist and how can these be mitigated?
- *Value proposition and sales presentation strategy.* What is our value proposition and what differentiates us from the competition? How does it solve a prospect's business challenges? Does it reduce expense, increase revenue or both? Can we prove this? What will increase customer interest and urgency?
- *Barriers to be overcome.* What are the barriers to sales success – competition from other companies, lack of confidence in the start-up or the new technology and so on? What are common objections? Who tends to express each objection and how will you resolve them in your

marketing and sales process? Do we need to educate before we can sell? What endorsement from respected authorities can we use to reassure prospects?

- *Alignment with marketing.* Are leads adequately nurtured and scored for sales readiness or should better routines be installed? What marketing efforts (e.g. promotions, events, discounting) are planned and how will these support the sales cycle? Is the timing correct? Will it create synergy? Which simple extra marketing or other support activities (e.g. better after-sales service, follow-up) are required?
- *Goal setting and target assignment.* What are your targets for new customer acquisition and existing customer sales? What sales activities will enable you to achieve these goals? What sales budget do you need to develop and implement these sales activities?
- *Sales staff and recruitment.* Are the sales staff well educated and competent or is more training required? Is sales capacity adequate or should extra people be hired, and if so, what qualifications and profile do they need? Will extra sales support the extra expenses? What recruitment actions will be taken?
- *Control.* Have activities been implemented well and are they effective? What can you learn from this evaluation? Should goals be retained or new goals be set?

Compared with the experimental mode of entrepreneurial selling, regular selling is less uncertain and more focused on persuading and ensuring that a created relationship will continue. Entrepreneurial selling requires an *adaptive selling* approach. Adaptive selling concerns 'the altering of sales behaviours during a customer interaction or across customer interactions based on perceived information about the nature of the selling situation'.[8] Adaptive selling is less monotonous than repeating the same message to all prospects, takes more concentration while interacting with prospects and requires more pre-call planning and information gathering. Such behaviour increases with experience, and in the context of selling an innovation requires both solid sales and technical knowhow of the salesperson.[9] A more seasoned and knowledgeable salesperson will be more inclined to connect to, and work with, the team of engineers developing the innovation. He or she will understand that experimentation and customer feedback are critical to the innovation's success. Therefore, such a salesperson is more likely to bring together research and development people from the start-up and venturous customers in order to help its engineers better understand the customers' needs and vantage point.

8.4 Developing the sales message

The sales message should prove to prospects that the start-up has an important new solution and advice to offer. A strong message uses a strong value proposition that delivers clear, tangible results such as increased revenues, decreased costs, improved operational efficiency and improved customer retention levels, among others. It should draw on the customer value and advantage of your start-up's new product. The boxed text that follows shows a basic format that you can use. It emphasises transferring knowledge about the product and explaining how the product links to the customer's situation and problems.

Your sales message needs to be short, clear and focused on the value the new product (or service) provides to customers of your target market. Thus, benefits rather than features or technology should be stressed. Observable features of the product can be mentioned and should be carefully linked to particular benefits. It will help the customer relate the product to his or her problem situation.

A basic format for a sales message

Our company, _____,
    offers to _____ (target customers)
    a new solution: _____ (concept → problem).
Our primary points of difference are _____.
Our main benefits include _____.
This is what our customers say about our product and us: _____ (references/testimonials).
With (our product), you (the customer) will be able to achieve (customer's goals) _____.

You should pitch the main message to the person in charge in the DMU of the potential customer. During the presentation and questions-and-answer session, it helps to address the needs of the prospect as fully as possible by showing understanding of their situation and by being responsive to all their questions. Furthermore, make sure all parties in the group feel involved. In fact, for every stakeholder in the DMU, a separate, solid, accurate, professional message should be developed. If a team is involved in pitching the start-up's new product, it pays to make sure that each individual contributes and understands his or her role.

Doing it right – Prepare sales presentations well

Companies always hold a debrief after a sales presentation and any member of the group who feels ignored can tip the scales in your disfavour. Once doubt and criticism about the product have been raised in the debrief, corporate group-think can take over. Your formerly stellar sales presentation can be shot full of holes when later, behind doors, staff are asked for their criticism. This means that you must obtain a list of all attendees and their functions in advance before you prepare your presentation and that clear and solid arguments should be developed for each stakeholder. Such a proactive approach can help ensure you move forward in the sales process and increases the chance of closing the deal. Moreover, even if you do not manage to make the sale, you will learn in the process from the feedback obtained.

Because start-ups need to prove themselves and may suddenly disappear from the market due to instability, it is important to pay particular attention to building trust in the start-up's future. References, support from investors, any prizes won and links with the scientific community or experts can be used for this. Growth in the start-up's sales may also be used as an indication of the attractiveness of its product, success and likelihood of survival.

If possible, you can demonstrate your high-tech product as part of the presentation. It is smart to try to involve your prospect in the demonstration, for instance, by asking them to operate the system or letting them choose options. It creates a bond and is one of the best ways to decrease scepticism. But practise this demonstration beforehand repeatedly, considering all the points that could malfunction. Nothing should be left to chance. A successful presentation covers all relevant details, but without boring the audience. Commit them to memory so that you can concentrate on the issues that arise from your customer. Of course, your audience will ask questions. If you do not know an answer, simply admit it, note it down, find out the answer and make sure you send a response to the entire group within 24 hours. Customers want to see and experience a responsive human being they can trust.

Doing it right – Three important guidelines for approaching your prospects

First, selling requires listening rather than hearing. The difference is understanding what the prospect says and being sensitive to his or her concerns and needs, and (jointly) looking for solutions. Listening thus is proactive and aimed at helping detect and resolve the customer's problem. It is a necessary trait for being able to establish whether your new product application will be a good option for the client.

Second, the sales message should focus on benefits rather than features, or even better, link features to benefits. This will help the prospect understand the product as a means to an end – why your new product is a solution to the customer's problem. In this process, existing alternatives in the marketplace may be used as benchmarks, illustrating how and why the new product is better.

Third, to stimulate the prospect of talking about his or her situation, you can use the SPIN model and sequence, which refers to situation, problem, implication and need–payoff of a customer:[10]

- *Situation questions.* First, ask about facts and background. This information helps you understand the customer's context and stage of development.
- *Problem questions.* Second, explore problems, difficulties and dissatisfactions in areas where your start-up's product can help.
- *Implication questions.* Third, follow up on a customer problem and explore its effects. The aim is to help the customer understand the problem's seriousness.
- *Need–payoff questions.* Finally, ask questions that encourage the customer to tell you the benefits that your solution could offer. You can use these clues to modify and refine your own sales message.

Previously, we saw that most new technologies enter a market from below; that is, most new technologies and their applications underperform, at least on some core dimensions, compared with existing products available on the market. Therefore, we should pay special attention to the order in which positive and negative claims are presented to customers. For true innovators (i.e. technology enthusiasts), this probably makes no or little difference. Attracted by the positive aspects of a new technology, they are not easily put off by the technology's drawbacks. For early adopters and the early majority, however, it is a different situation. Early adopters, and particularly the early majority, make more rational evaluations than innovators. Consequently, the order of arguments may make a difference in the way these customers weigh positives and negatives. Much will depend on the severity of the negatives. If the negatives are minor, the order may again not matter much. However, if – often in the case with new technology – the negatives are serious, it is better to address them first and get them out of the way. With the negatives out of the way, all attention can focus on the positive points. The advantage is that you now can close with a positive message, leaving the customer with a positive feeling.[11]

8.5 Managing customer expectations

A start-up developing a new technology and application often experiences important setbacks and delays. While in the beginning, sales for a start-up may be hard because there is no physical product to show to the customer, delays in final product design and production are other elements that can be accounted for and anticipated. Unexpected delays may leave customers frustrated and create negative word of mouth.

This explains why managing customer expectations is an essential element of the customer relationship development process. Customers understand that new ventures face a lot of uncertainty and thus that delays can occur. However, they do expect you to handle matters professionally. As soon as they think you are not in control, disappointment and even anger may arise. As boundary functions, marketing and sales are most affected and should take charge. Here are some tips to keep customers satisfied.

First, it is important to underpromise and overperform. It is better to set reasonable goals and exceed a customer's expectations than to promise the world and underdeliver. Make sure you can consistently achieve and exceed by setting realistic expectations with customers. If for some reason you cannot meet goals, cushion with empathy and be open about the situation and problems. Tell it as it is. This is least painful and creates a new basis to work from. Acknowledging the customer's issue and relating to their emotions through empathetic listening will provide psychological compensation and soften customers' reaction.

Second, it is important to understand the customer's priorities. Ask questions to make sure you understand the customers' needs and timeline. This will allow assessment of whether you can still fulfil their wishes despite the delay. For those customers who are willing to wait, determine their expectations and make new arrangements. For those customers who cannot be kept on board, you should make alternative arrangements, for example, by offering them a refund.

To be able to respond to problems and customer inquiries effectively, you need to develop excellent service procedures. Here also the adage of underpromise and overperform applies. Although you may explain on your website that you will respond in, for instance, two days, you will make a better and lasting impression if you respond in half the time.

Example – CTRL Eyewear's handling of delay

An example of good expectation management is CTRL Eyewear.[12] Established in 2015 in the Netherlands as a subsidiary of Alpha-Micron Inc., a firm with vast experience in adaptive military lens technology, CTRL Eyewear designs, develops and markets innovative eyewear. It sells lightning fast e-Tint technology glasses targeting high-performance athletes and outdoor adventurists. These glasses immediately switch from bright to shade depending on the light situation. A promotion film starring cyclist Andy Schleck illustrates how the product works (www.youtube.com/watch?v= Sy97UdWIUkM; accessed 16 December 2016).

After CTRL Eyewear was bought by AlphaMicron, the decision was made to move production to the USA. Although this benefited product quality, customer expectations regarding delivery could not be met. CTRL Eyewear asked the customers who had bought the glasses upfront on the Internet in a crowdfunding action whether they minded waiting. Most customers did not mind the delay, but some customers who had bought the new product planning to use it as a Christmas gift were disappointed. To cater to these customers' needs, the firm offered an apology and a quick refund.

Summary

- Entrepreneurial selling is characterised by high uncertainty and involves a sales learning process and serious knowledge brokering. The process is difficult to accelerate. Only when sales accelerate should the sales force be extended.

- A good integration between the sales staff and the engineering team developing the new technology and application is important. It will help customer relationship development by the start-up's salesperson(s).
- Allocate resources to identify prospects and move them through the buying cycle. Maintain and extend existing customer relationships to begin building a customer portfolio. Adaptive selling is required.
- Develop a sales presentation by paying close attention to different members of the customer's DMU; deliver a convincing message for all people involved. Focus on conveying the unique business value of your product for the customer.

Notes

1 Blank (2007: 214).
2 Leslie and Holloway (2006).
3 Berg *et al.* (2013).
4 Higgins *et al.* (2003).
5 Jasmand *et al.* (2012).
6 Kuester *et al.* (2016).
7 For instance, Geery and Barrieau (2011).
8 Weitz *et al.* (1986: 175).
9 Franke and Park (2006).
10 Rackham (1995).
11 Based on Cialdini (2014).
12 BNR Radio – interview with Daf E. Dubbelman, CEO CTRL Eyewear (Presenting at Harvard, 13 October 2015).

Chapter 9

Developing the new firm's marketing and sales capabilities

Key issues

- Explain the importance of developing marketing and sales capabilities to achieve competitive advantage.
- Discuss how different capabilities are required for survival (customer discovery and validation) and growth (customer creation and company development).
- Explain marketing's contribution to different business processes.
- Identify a total set of marketing capabilities.

9.1 Developing the commercial capabilities of the new firm

The resource-based view asserts that firms gain and sustain competitive advantage by developing and using the organisation's resources. These resources refer to tangible and intangible assets, and are used in *business processes* contributing to the implementation of a start-up's strategy. Business processes are actions that firms rely on to accomplish some business purpose or objective.[1] They act as the routines or activities that a firm develops in order to get something done and reach its objectives. Examples are developing new products, supply chain management to manufacture and deliver products and attracting new and maintaining relationships with existing customers.

A firm is the sum of its business processes. When these are well aligned, the resulting synergy creates greater value than the sum of each individual process. Therefore, entrepreneurs should avoid suboptimisation of the business processes by focusing on some processes and neglecting others.

Resources are used in business processes and become firm capabilities. Firm capabilities are skills or abilities to make things happen for an organisation. Excellent capabilities are difficult for competitors to copy and thus form the foundation of a firm's customer value and competitive advantage in the market. Therefore, developing these capabilities is of the utmost importance. Developing firm capabilities is relevant to all business processes. For instance, a firm should not only create capabilities to develop its new products technically, but also create strong capabilities in marketing and sales to ensure the new product's commercialisation.

The first capabilities an entrepreneur needs are the ability to identify the market opportunity, develop the business plan and attract funding. After that, attention will shift towards developing the new firm's product, developing its organisation and building a customer base. While some level of innovation and marketing capabilities may be present, the need to develop them further will increase after the plans have been finalised and venture capital secured. Then, innovation capabilities and marketing capabilities need to be developed and added.

Bell and Mason[2] created a model to help start-ups in their capability development process. Based on experience with hundreds of ventures, they created a web model emphasising the required shifts of focus. Their model has been embraced by Philips Electronics, for example, for developing its lab ventures. The model (see Figure 9.1) includes 12 dimensions and 4 stages of development of the start-up that closely match the main stages of the new product development trajectory:

1 concept or conceptualisation of product and business model;
2 seeding money or funding;
3 product development; and
4 market development.

The 12 dimensions refer (using abbreviated labels) to the types of capabilities that every start-up needs. They vary from product (or product concept), business plan (development), marketing, sales, manufacturing, research and development (R&D)/engineering or new product development, to attracting funds, engaging in teamwork, CEO quality and administrative control capabilities. The model illustrates which organisational dimensions or capabilities should be developed and available at each stage. Bell and Mason explain that in the beginning, in the conceptualisation phase (between 0 and 1), entrepreneurs' attention should focus on making a business plan, technology engineering and generating funding. At this conceptualisation phase, marketing and sales are important for identifying

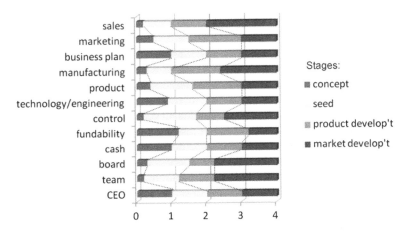

Figure 9.1 Impression of the Bell–Mason diagram of ideal state of capabilities at each stage of the start-up's development (adapted from Bell and McNamara 1991)

the market and market potential, but their actual roles are limited. So, limited levels of marketing and sales capabilities suffice at this stage.

Next, in the seed phase ([more or less] between 1 and 2), the entrepreneur should look for venture capital and persuade investors to support his or her idea. As Figure 9.1 indicates, here again, modest marketing and sales knowledge is sufficient. However, during the product development phase, things change ([more or less] between 2 and 3). Now, sales gains importance and marketing becomes a dominant force. It can be explained by the new firm's need to discover (and validate) customers for its innovation or product application, preferably before much money is spent on developing a prototype. It implies that serious investments in marketing resources are now needed. The entrepreneur should make sure that the necessary marketing and sales capabilities have been built to allow for this input.

The final stage of the Bell–Mason model concerns market development (between 3 and 4) and gives a key role to sales. This phase resembles Blank's business building.[3] At this stage of development, all attention should shift towards scaling up the business. This process requires rapid improvement of the organisation's sales capabilities, while marketing has a more modest support role.[4]

The Bell–Mason model offers a general understanding of the 12 important capabilities a start-up should develop. Although each capability's importance shifts at different stages of the start-up's evolution, we would like to stress that at all times, the capability profile of the firm is a balanced mix of them.

Developing capabilities in a timely fashion is important to enable the start-up to switch to the next development stage with its required configuration of capabilities. For instance, one may develop a plan for a new business but should not forget that the ability to make a convincing pitch is critical to obtain funding. In a similar way, it is important to get the product to work properly and to resolve technical issues, but this should not distract the firm from developing its commercial skills or from resolving manufacturing and supply chain issues.

In a recent study, Ngo and O'Cass[5] argued that a firm that is focused on market developments will build better innovation and marketing capabilities. These firms also have more successful new product development outcomes. The authors showed that for obtaining maximum customer value levels of the new product, technical and marketing capabilities should work together, that is, be combined and integrated. Such integration benefits the customer performance of the newly developed product as well as the firm's financial performance. Aligning technical and marketing capabilities in the product development stage of the start-up serves this purpose. Simultaneous investments in engineering and marketing capabilities facilitate simultaneous technical product development as well as discovery and validation of customer demand.

Although the Bell–Mason model does not differentiate between effectual and traditional marketing and sales capabilities, it is easy to understand that attention will shift from company survival to company growth. The degree to which effectual or traditional marketing/sales should be used and the speed of the shift from one to another will depend on the level of newness of the product and how quickly a foothold in the market is created. Compared with radical new products, incremental new products will require less effectual marketing and sales. If market entry is obtained quickly, a swift switch from effectuation to traditional marketing and sales can be made. Yet, it is also clear that Bell and Mason link marketing rather than sales with customer discovery and validation, and associated company building with sales rather than marketing. In contrast, we adopted a more balanced perspective.

9.2 Marketing and sales capabilities for survival and growth stages

Although research supports the positive effect of marketing and sales capabilities on firm performance,[6] for start-ups a more detailed perspective is useful. Start-ups need to focus on survival before they can focus on growing their business. *Survival* refers to discovering customers and validating their interest in the new product, and possibly changing the product to better satisfy these customers' (latent) needs. *Growth* concerns expanding the customer segment and base. It concerns company development and leveraging the marketing and sales roadmap that has been developed. Consistent with this, we differentiate between marketing and sales capabilities that are particularly useful in each of these two stages. Effectual marketing is most suited to be used in the beginning of the start-up's existence, that is, for customer discovery/validation. Traditional marketing is best used for customer creation and particularly for company building. Figure 9.2 shows a start-up's commercialisation efforts and the effect on the two outcomes of the different stages of development.[7] The level of effort is anticipated to be moderated positively or negatively by different marketing and sales capabilities. The effectual-related factors, which are shown in the top row, mainly benefit survival, whereas the traditional marketing capabilities, shown in the bottom row, cater to growth. The set of factors or capabilities listed is illustrative rather than exhaustive. The effectual factor of 'market probing and experimentation', for example, is anticipated as useful for start-ups, but also for established firms that want to grow using not incremental but more radical innovations. This explains why a positive effect is expected for both survival and growth. The factors of regular market research and account management, however, expect positively moderate growth but negatively influence the commercialisation efforts' effect on survival. Regular market research is generally considered too limited in scope and, as a result, leads to uninformed and even wrong decisions due to its reliance on existing market boundaries and product categories. Similar arguments apply to the effect of account management and other regular marketing variables.

So, when a start-up targets its first market segment, it is faced with the tasks of creating entirely new routines and developing its marketing and sales capabilities. These are resource-intensive processes that require substantial investments. Examples of marketing/sales capabilities that benefit survival, and thus, that should be developed, are: (1) buzz marketing to build presence in the marketplace as well as create awareness for the new product application; (2) experimentation with customers to discover and validate demand; (3) networking to find the right business partners and marketing channel to gain access to the market (i.e. customers); and (4) basic pricing skills. These capabilities clearly relate to effectual marketing. Four capabilities that align with the growth stage of firm development can also be identified. These involve regular or traditional marketing capabilities. Having passed the so-called valley of death and thus having established the validity of its new product, the firm can begin using

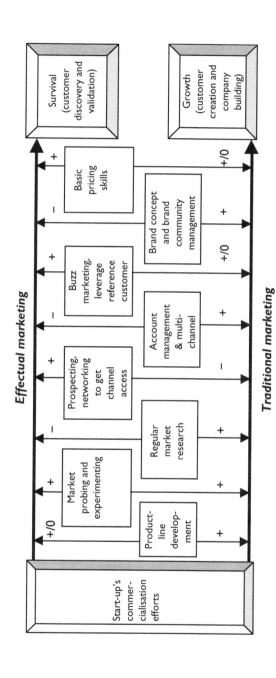

Figure 9.2 Marketing and sales capabilities and the effects on survival and growth

more regular marketing and sales capabilities. These include, for instance, (1) account management; (2) communication with, and development of, the firm's brand community and brand; (3) development of the firm's product line; and (4) engagement in regular market research.

The transformation from survival to growth (and thus from effectual to regular marketing) generally is incremental because dealing with uncertainty slowly gives way to the exploration of the start-up's new markets as knowledge and experience accumulate. The greater the firm's accumulation of experience and sales, the more resource commitment the entrepreneur can make to build marketing and sales capabilities, switching from one approach to the other.

9.3 Marketing capabilities' specific contribution to business processes

Recognising customers as the ultimate arbiters of the value a firm creates and the value its product and technology represent, managers have increasingly recognised the importance of marketing and sales capabilities for firms' success.[8] Marketing and sales capabilities play an important role in aligning a firm with its market. Marketing and sales capabilities particularly contribute to business processes of (1) new product development; (2) customer relationship management; and (3) supply chain management.[9]

Because of entrepreneurs' focus on innovation, we begin by highlighting the connection of marketing and sales capabilities to the new product (service) development process. Cooper[10] noted a great many marketing tasks that should be performed to ensure positive innovation process outcomes. Figure 9.3 shows the different technical and marketing activities necessary. The execution and quality of these marketing activities for the start-up will depend on the presence of marketing and sales capabilities within the new firm. Even if outsourced, some expertise will be necessary to ensure the quality of the work by hiring the right people. The early tasks relate to customer discovery and validation, whereas the later tasks involve product launch and sales. These marketing activities, although here considered part of product development, clearly also have relationships with customer development and management. This relationship is shown on the right-hand side of the figure.

As the new firm becomes established, its organisation will evolve and grow. It will result in more formal functions and processes. While marketing (or new customer development) and supply chain activities are first organised around the new product development of the start-up, the activities become increasingly important and institutionalised. Thus, they become recognisable as separate and regular business processes. With

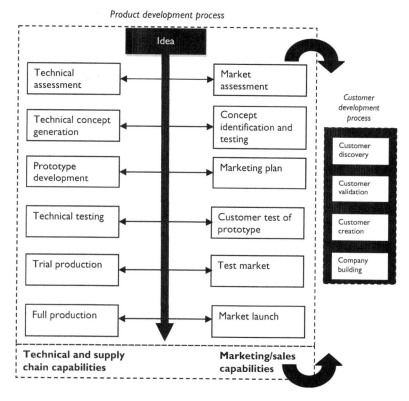

Figure 9.3 Technical and marketing activities in new product development (adapted from Cooper 1983) and the relationship with the customer development process

existing customers repurchasing the product and new customers adding to the firm's overall sales, the customer base is expanding. As a result of this, attention will shift from prospecting towards maintaining customer relationships. In a similar way, the need for more formal supply chain management will evolve. If we look at Figure 9.3, we note that the final steps of the new product development process refer to trial and full production, respectively. For such production runs, efficient manufacturing processes and a supply chain with necessary logistics should have been developed. It suggests a link to and presence of a supply chain process.

Based on the previous section, Figure 9.4 recognises and integrates all three processes from a marketing and sales resources perspective.

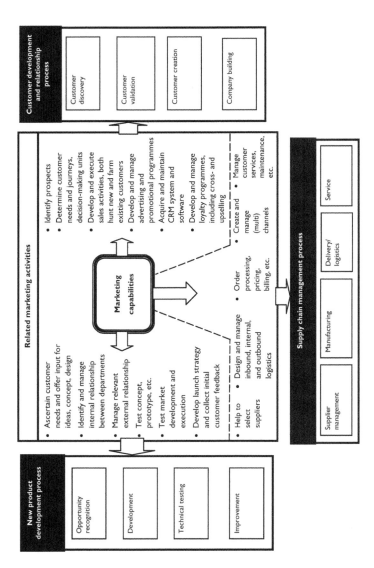

Customer development and relationship process

- Customer discovery
- Customer validation
- Customer creation
- Company building

Related marketing activities

- Ascertain customer needs and offer input for ideas, concept, design
- Identify and manage internal relationship between departments
- Manage relevant external relationship
- Test concept, prototype, etc.
- Test market development and execution
- Develop launch strategy and collect initial customer feedback

Marketing capabilities

- Identify prospects
- Determine customer needs and journeys, decision-making units
- Develop and execute sales activities, both hunt new and farm existing customers
- Develop and manage advertising and promotional programmes
- Acquire and maintain CRM system and software
- Develop and manage loyalty programmes, including cross- and upselling
- Create and manage (multi) channels
- Manage customer services, maintenance, etc.

- Order processing, pricing, billing, etc.

- Help to select suppliers
- Design and manage inbound, internal, and outbound logistics

New product development process

- Opportunity recognition
- Development
- Technical testing
- Improvement

Supply chain management process

- Supplier management
- Manufacturing
- Delivery/ logistics
- Service

Figure 9.4 Integrated perspective of marketing capabilities, activities and business processes (adapted from Srivastava *et al.* 1999)

It shows new product development, customer development and relationship management and supply chain management, and illustrates the link with important marketing and sales activities. The level of the underlying marketing and sales capabilities determines the quality of these activities achieved.

Marketing and sales capabilities can be developed by educating and training engineers, or by hiring specialised staff. Engineers with commercial training and marketers or salespeople with a technical background are preferred because they can easily navigate between technical and commercial issues. Understanding both the technical and commercial side of things, they are in an ideal situation to interact with customers, but they also help the start-up's own engineers to improve the current product solution if necessary. They can explain to the start-up's engineers how to change the product as they can think about customer benefit but also along technological dimensions.

The number of marketing/sales people required at the early stage of development is an empirical question, but is rarely seriously considered in many start-ups. The appropriate numbers of marketing, sales and engineering staff should be determined by the set of marketing and sales capabilities needed.

In addition, investments in building marketing information systems (MIS) will be necessary. This also contributes to the firm's marketing capabilities. It involves generating, analysing and disseminating information about customers and competitors, but also about other stakeholders who are important to the start-up's business. A customer relationship management (CRM) module may be part of the firm's MIS.

Finally, a firm will develop a full-fledged set of marketing (and sales) capabilities. It will include capabilities to perform marketing analyses at strategic and tactical levels, ranging from branding to pricing decisions. Table 9.1 offers a general overview of these capabilities.

9.4 Implement, evaluate and improve the one-page marketing and sales plan

To secure a proper organisational development, the start-up needs a strong, viable marketing and sales function. This can be accomplished by investing in marketing and sales capabilities, but is sustained by the ability of these functions to *act accountably* and thus show how they contribute to the start-up's bottom line. By developing marketing and sales performance measures, a greater status for marketing and sales can be achieved. It will secure future investment in marketing and sales capabilities. It will

Table 9.1 Sample of marketing-relevant subprocesses in the main business processes (adapted from Srivastava et al. 1999)

Product development management process	Supply chain management process	Customer relationship management process
Ascertain customer needs and offer input for ideas, concept, design	Help select suppliers	Identify prospects
Identify and manage internal relationship between departments	Design and manage inbound, internal and outbound logistics	Determine customer needs and buying process, decision-making units
Manage relevant external relationship	Order processing, pricing, billing, etc.	Develop and execute sales activities, both prospecting and account management
Test concept, prototype, etc.	Create and manage (multi) channels	Develop and manage advertising and promotional programmes
Test market development and execution	Manage customer services, maintenance, etc.	Acquire and maintain CRM system and software
Develop launch strategy and collect initial customer feedback		Develop and manage loyalty programmes, including cross- and upselling

also free up resources to ensure that the firm's future products will be developed with the customer and market in mind. This is important, as chasms may always potentially occur and slow down the start-up's development.

The simple marketing and sales plans used at the beginning of the development of the start-up will slowly but surely become more elaborate and detailed. When this happens, effectuation will be replaced by traditional or causal marketing planning efforts. Consistent with this, the collection and analysis of market data will become more standardised and the relationship with important marketing and sales decisions more routine. A 'marketing dashboard' can be developed. A dashboard is a refined set of marketing performance data, usually presented together, which provides an overview of the strategic marketing performance of the firm.[11] Two important elements of dashboards are that they provide automated or virtually real-time reporting and that they offer their users indicators and levers to make the changes necessary to optimise outcomes. Possible indicators of overall marketing performance are, for instance, sales volume per month and year, profit margin and market share or share of (the customer's) wallet. Specific indicators, referring to individual marketing instruments and levers, may include the effectiveness of promotions, customer satisfaction and loyalty, quality of distribution and after-sales service performance (recovery speed, customer satisfaction after repair, etc.), but also the number of new leads, lead conversion rate and percentage sales to existing and to new customers. Levers are the product, the brand of the company, and its distribution and relationship management strategy, among others.[12]

The presence of a marketing dashboard helps marketing and sales people to enhance the effect of their efforts. And, although at first the scope of the marketing dashboard will be limited, start-ups will benefit and can enhance the credibility of their marketing efforts by developing such a tool.

9.5 Concluding remarks

Over 40 years ago, Drucker stressed the importance for firms of investing in marketing and sales alongside developing new products.[13] Otherwise, the new product's market success might be hampered. His advice was based on observations that firms generally underspend during concept development and launch, which jeopardised the chance of generating customer interest and creating customer demand.

Another captain of industry advocated a similar message. The steel tycoon Andrew Carnegie once said: 'You can take away my money, you can take away my factories, but leave me my sales staff, and I will be back where I was in two years.'[14] His quote stressed the strategic value of sales and the importance of control over a firm's customer assets. Only with a strong value proposition and strong sales capabilities will a firm be able to sustain itself.

Of course, there also is anecdotal evidence suggesting that marketing and sales are not important. For instance, in a radio interview, the successful Dutch entrepreneur Raymond Cloosterman, CEO of Rituals (a new brand of innovative personal body-care products), claimed that his success had nothing to do with smart marketing and sales. However, such claims are misleading as even a cursory evaluation of this start-up's success shows excellent rather than no marketing and sales capabilities.

The examples of the previous section suggest that firms benefit from excellent marketing and sales. Particularly if a start-up gets both its product/R&D and marketing/sales right, it will enjoy success. So, entrepreneurs should make sure to develop the technological and commercial capabilities of their new firm if they want to survive and grow effectively. What can help is distinguishing a customer development process next to the product development process and appointing a product and a customer development team. Entrepreneurs who manage and bridge these two processes effectively are true artists and will enjoy higher success rates.

Compared with Drucker's general observations, recent marketing and entrepreneurial literature has evolved and offers a large set of useful ideas and tools. The book you are currently reading combined many of these up-to-date insights into a single framework. Placing the effectual view at centre stage, it emphasised that beginning with new technology and product application, an entrepreneur can search for the optimal environment and optimum target segment to enter the market and to grow. However, this is not a simple sequential process, but an iterative and continuing process that requires involving potential customers as soon as possible. Many complications and mistakes can be prevented by discovering and validating demand quickly, before making serious investments in developing an actual, working prototype. And, although some start-ups have survived using a business model that relies on sponsors and advertising revenue, for most start-ups, paying customers are key to their survival and growth. This book can help accomplish that goal.

Summary

- Start-ups should carefully develop their marketing and sales capabilities in a timely way. It requires investing in marketing and sales staff.
- First, marketing and sales capabilities need to be shaped in accordance with the effectuation view and focus on helping to achieve survival.
- Next, attention should shift to building marketing and sales capabilities to grow the business.
- Developing marketing and sales capabilities is a vital part of creating a complete organisation that is able to manage the interface with the customer in all it aspects.
- Marketing and sales capabilities contribute not only to new product development, but also to customer management and supply chain management processes.

Notes

1 Ray *et al.* (2004).
2 See Bell and McNamara (1991); and, for example, http://astraea.net/blog/?
   p=1883 (accessed 16 December 2016).
3 Blank (2007).
4 Bell and McNamara (1991).
5 Ngo and O'Cass (2012).
6 Morgan *et al.* (2009).
7 Inspired by Sapienza *et al.* (2006).
8 Priem (2007).
9 Srivastava *et al.* (1999, 2001).
10 Cooper (1983).
11 O'Sullivan and Abela (2007).
12 Rust *et al.* (2000).
13 Drucker (1973: 785).
14 See www.icmrindia.org/courseware/Sales%20Management/Sales%20
   Management.htm (accessed 16 December 2016).

References

Abell, D. (1980), *Defining the Business: The Starting Point of Strategic Planning*, Prentice Hall, Englewood Cliffs, NJ.

Allen, K. (2010), *Entrepreneurship for Scientists and Engineers*, Prentice Hall, Upper Saddle River, NJ.

Ansoff, H. I. (1984), *Implanting Strategic Management*, Prentice Hall, London, UK.

Atuahene-Gima, K. and Evangelista, F. (2000), Cross-functional influence in new product development: an exploratory study of marketing and R&D perspectives, *Management Science*, 46(10), 1269–84.

Baron, R. A. and Ensley, M. D. (2006), Opportunity recognition as the detection of meaningful patterns: evidence from comparisons of novice and experienced entrepreneurs, *Management Science*, 52(9), 1331–44.

Bell, C. G. and McNamara, J. (1991), *High Tech Ventures: A Guide to Entrepreneurial Success*, Addison Wesley, Reading, MA.

Berg, W. E. van den, Rietdijk, W. J. R., Verbeke, W. J. M. I., Bagozzi, R. P., Worm, L., de Jong, A. and Nijssen, E. J. (2013), *Salespersons as Internal Knowledge Brokers and New Product Selling: Uncovering a Link to Genetic Makeup*, Working Paper, Erasmus University Rotterdam, Rotterdam, The Netherlands.

Blank, S. G. (2007), *The Four Steps to the Epiphany: Successful Strategies for Products that Win*, 4th revised edn, Lulu Enterprises, Raleigh, NC.

Bommel, T. van (2010), 'Radical New Project Management for Developing Radical New Product Applications', Master's Thesis, Eindhoven University of Technology, Eindhoven, The Netherlands.

Bommel, T. van, Mahieu, R. J. and Nijssen, E. J. (2014), Technology trajectories and the selection of optimal R&D project sequences, *IEEE Transactions on Engineering Management*, 61(4), 669–80.

Charness, N., Reingold, E. M., Pomplun, M. and Stampe, D. M. (2001), The perceptual aspect of skilled performance in chess: evidence from eye movements, *Memory & Cognition*, 29(8), 1146–52.

Christensen, C. M. (1997), *The Innovator's Dilemma*, HBS Press, Boston, MA.

Cialdini, R. (2014), Keynote on influence tactics in sales, Thought Leadership on the Sales Profession Conference, 10–11 June, Columbia University, New York, NY.

Cooper, R. G. (1983), A process model for industrial new product development, *IEEE Transactions on Engineering Management*, EM30(1), 2–11.

Coviello, N. E. and Joseph, R. M. (2012), Creating major innovations with customers: insights from small and young technology firms, *Journal of Marketing*, 76(6), 87–104.

DeKinder, J. S. and Kohli, A. K. (2008), Flow signals: how patterns over time affect the acceptance of start-up firms, *Journal of Marketing*, 72(5), 84–97.

DiBenedetto, A. (1999), Identifying the key success factors in new product launch, *Journal of Product Innovation Management*, 16(6), 530–44.

Dijk, S. van, Berends, H., Jelinek, M., Romme, A. G. L. and Weggeman, M. (2011), Micro-institutional affordances and strategies of radical innovations, *Organization Studies*, 32(11), 1485–513.

Dimov, D. and de Clerck, D. (2006), Venture capital investment strategy and portfolio failure rate: a longitudinal study, *Entrepreneurship Theory and Practice*, 30(2), 207–23.

Dmitriev, V., Simmons, G., Truong, Y., Palmer, M. and Schneckenberg, D. (2014), An exploration of business model development in the commercialization of technology innovations, *R&D Management*, 44(3), 306–21.

Drucker, P. F. (1973), *Management: Tasks, Responsibilities, Practices*, Harper and Row, New York, NY.

Drucker, P. F. (1985), The discipline of innovation, *Harvard Business Review*, 63(3), 67–72.

Ehret, M., Kashyap, V. and Wirtz, J. (2013), Business models: impact on business markets and opportunities for marketing research, *Industrial Marketing Management*, 42(5), 649–55.

Fogel, S., Hoffmeister, D., Rocco, R. and Strunk, D. P. (2012), Teaching sales, *Harvard Business Review*, 90(7), 94–9.

Franke, G. R. and Park, J. E. (2006), Salesperson adaptive selling behavior and customer orientation: a meta-analysis, *Journal of Marketing Research*, 43(4), 693–702.

Fuchs, C. and Schreier, M. (2011), Customer empowerment in new product development, *Journal of Product Innovation Management*, 28(1), 17–32.

Garcia, R. and Atkin, T. (2002), *Coo-petition for the Diffusion of Resistant Innovations: A Case Study in the Global Wine Industry*, Working Paper, Institute for Global Innovation Management, 05–002, 1–22.

Geery, B. and Barrieau, T. (2011), *Sales Productivity Architects Corporate Website*, available online at http://salesproductivityarchitects.com (accessed 9 September 2013).

Gourville, J. T. (2006), Eager sellers, stony buyers: understanding the psychology of new-product adoption, *Harvard Business Review*, 84(6), 99–106.

Griffin, A., Hoffmann, N., Price, R. L. and Voljak, B. A. (2007), *How Serial Innovators Navigate the Fuzzy Front End of New Product Development*, ISBM Report 3–2007, The Institute for the Study of Business Markets, University Park, PA.

Gruber, M., MacMillan, I. C. and Thompson, J. D. (2008), Look before you leap: market opportunity identification in emerging technology firms, *Management Science*, 54(9), 1652–65.

Guiltinan, J. P. (1999), Launch strategy, launch tactics, and demand outcomes, *Journal of Product Innovation Management*, 16(6), 509–29.

Higgins, E. T., Kruglanski, A. W. and Pierro, A. (2003), Regulatory mode: locomotion and assessment as distinct orientations, in: Zanna, M. P. (ed.), *Advances in Experimental Social Psychology*, Academic Press, New York, NY, pp. 293–344.

Hikmet, R. A. M. and Bommel, T. van (2006), Active beam manipulation, in: Aarts, E. and Diederiks, E. (eds), *Ambient Lifestyle: From Concept to Experience*, BIS Publishers and Bright, Amsterdam, The Netherlands, pp. 195–7.

Hippel, E. von (1986), Lead users: a source of novel product concepts, *Management Science*, 32(7), 791–805.

Hoffman, D. L., Kopalle, P. K. and Novak, Th. P. (2010), The 'right' consumers for better concepts: identifying consumers high in emergent nature to develop new product concepts, *Journal of Marketing Research*, 47(5), 854–65.

Hooley, G. J., Saunders, J. A. and Piercy, N. F. (1998), *Marketing Strategy and Competitive Positioning*, Prentice Hall International, Hemel Hempstead, UK.

Huchzermeier, A. and Loch, C. H. (2001), Project management under risk: using the real options approach to evaluate flexibility in R&D, *Management Science*, 47(1), 85–101.

Jasmand, C., Blazevic, V. and de Ruyter, K. (2012), Generating sales while providing service: a study of customer service representatives' ambidextrous behavior, *Journal of Marketing*, 76(1), 20–37.

Kleijnen, M., Lee, N. and Wetzels, M. (2009), An exploration of consumer resistance to innovation and its antecedents, *Journal of Economic Psychology*, 30(3), 344–57.

Kotler, P. and Keller, K. L. (2006), *Marketing Management*, 12th edn, Pearson, Prentice Hall, Upper Saddle River, NJ.

Kuester, S., Homburg, C. and Hildesheim, A. (2016), The catbird seat of the sales force: how sales force integration leads to new product success, *International Journal of Research in Marketing*, doi: 10.1016/j.ijresmar.2016.08.008.

Lafley, A. G. (2004), Delivering delight, *Fast Talk*, 83(June), 51.

Laurila, J. and Lilja, K. (2002), The dominance of firm-level competitive pressures over functional-level institutional pressures: the case of the Finnish-based forest industry firms, *Organization Studies*, 23(4), 571–97.

Lee, Y. and O'Connor, G. C. (2003), New product launch strategy for network effects products, *Journal of the Academy of Marketing Science*, 31(3), 241–55.

Leslie, M. and Holloway, C. A. (2006), The sales learning curve, *Harvard Business Review*, 84(7/8), 115–23.

Li, T. and Calantone, R. J. (1998), The impact of market knowledge competence on new product advantage: conceptualization and empirical examination, *Journal of Marketing*, 62(4), 13–29.

Lynn, G. S., Morone, J. G. and Paulson, A. S. (1996), Marketing and discontinuous innovation: the probe and learn process, *California Management Review*, 38(3), 8–37.

Magretta, J. (2002), Why business models matter, *Harvard Business Review*, 80(5), 86–92.

Markides, C. (1998), Strategic innovation in established companies, *Sloan Management Review*, 39(3), 31–42.

Molesworth, M. and Suortti, J. P. (2002), Buying cars online: the adoption of the web for high-involvement, high cost purchases, *Journal of Consumer Behaviour*, 2(2), 155–68.

Moore, G. (2006), *Crossing the Chasm: Marketing and Selling High-Tech Products to Mainstream Customers*, Collins Business Essentials, New York, NY.

Moorman, C. and Rust, R. (1999), The role of marketing, *Journal of Marketing*, 63(special issue), 180–97.

Morgan, N. A., Slotegraaf, R. J. and Vorhies, D. W. (2009), Linking marketing capabilities with profit growth, *International Journal of Research in Marketing*, 26(4), 284–93.

Mullins, O., Walker, J., Boyd, H. and Larréché, J. (2005), *Marketing Management: A Strategic Decision-Making Approach*, 5th edn, McGraw-Hill, New York, NY.

Ngo, L. V. and O'Cass, A. (2012), In search of innovation and customer-related performance superiority: the role of market orientation, marketing capability, and innovation capability interactions, *Journal of Product Innovation Management*, 29(5), 861–77.

Nijssen, E. J., Hillebrand, B., de Jong, J. P. J. and Kemp, R. G. M. (2012), Strategic value assessment and explorative learning opportunities with customers, *Journal of Product Innovation Management*, 29(S1), 91–102.

O'Connor, G. C. and Rice, M. P. (2013), New market creation for breakthrough innovations: Enabling and constraining mechanisms, *Journal of Product Innovation Management*, 30(2), 209–27.

Onyemah, V., Rivera Pesquera, M. and Ali, A. (2013), What entrepreneurs get wrong, *Harvard Business Review*, 91(5), 74–9.

O'Sullivan, D. and Abela, A. V. (2007), Marketing performance measurement ability and firm performance, *Journal of Marketing*, 71(April), 79–93.

Popovic, D. R. and Fahrni, F. (2004), Launching the first mass product of a high-tech start-up company, Engineering Management Conference, *Proceedings of 2004 IEEE International*, 3, 929–33.

Porter, M. E. (1980), *Competitive Strategy: Techniques for Analyzing Industries and Competitors*, Free Press, New York, NY.

Priem, R. L. (2007), A consumer perspective on value creation, *Academy of Management Review*, 32(1), 219–35.

Rackham, N. (1995), *SPIN-Selling*, Gower Publishing, Aldershot, UK.

Ray, G., Barney, J. B. and Muhanna, W. A. (2004), Capabilities, business processes, and competitive advantage: choosing the dependent variable in empirical tests of the resource-based view, *Strategic Management Journal*, 25(1), 23–37.

Read, S., Dew, N., Sarasvathy, S. D., Song, M. and Wiltbank, R. (2009), Marketing under uncertainty: the logic of an effectual approach, *Journal of Marketing*, 73(3), 1–18.

Ries, A. and Trout, J. (1980), *Positioning: the battle for your Mind*, McGraw-Hill, New York, NY.

Rindova, V. P. and Petkova, A. P. (2007), When is a new thing a good thing? Technological change, product form design, and perceptions of value for product innovations, *Organization Science*, 18(2), 217–32.

Rogers, E. M. (2003), *Diffusion of Innovation*, Free Press, New York, NY.

Rosa, J. A., Porac, J. F., Runser-Spanjol, J. and Saxon, M. S. (1999), Sociocognitive dynamics in a product market, *Journal of Marketing*, 63(special issue), 64–77.

Rosen, E. (2002), *The Anatomy of Buzz: How to Create Word of Mouth Marketing*, Doubleday, Random House, New York, NY.

Ruokolainen, J. I. and Igel, B. (2004), The factors of making the first successful customer reference to leverage the business of start-up software company – multiple case studying Thai software industry, *Technovation*, 24(9), 673–81.

Rust, R. T., Zeithaml, V. A. and Lemon, K. N. (2000), *Driving Customer Equity: How Customer Lifetime Value is Reshaping Corporate Strategy*, The Free Press, New York, NY.

Salminen, R. T. and Möller, K. (2006), Role of references in business marketing: towards a normative theory of referencing, *Journal of Business to Business Marketing*, 13(1), 1–51.

Sapienza, H. J., Autio, E., George, G. and Zhara, S. A. (2006), A capabilities perspective on the effects of early internationalization on firm survival and growth, *Academy of Management Review*, 31(4), 914–33.

Shane, S. (2000), Prior knowledge and the discovery of entrepreneurial opportunities, *Organization Science*, 11(4), 448–69.

Simonin, B. L. and Ruth, J. A. (1998), Is a company known by the company it keeps? Assessing the spillover effects of brand alliances on consumer brand attitudes, *Journal of Marketing Research*, 35(1), 30–42.

Srinivasan, R., Lilien, G. L., Rangaswamy, A., Pingitore, G. M. and Seldin, D. (2012), The total product design concept and an application to the auto market, *Journal of Product Innovation Management*, 29(S1), 3–20.

Srivastava, R., Fahey, K. L. and Christensen, H. K. (2001), The resource-based view and marketing: the role of market-based assets in gaining competitive advantage, *Journal of Management*, 27(6), 777–802.

Srivastava, R. K., Shervani, T. A., and Fahey, L. (1999), Marketing, business processes, and shareholder value: an organizationally embedded view of marketing activities and the discipline of marketing, *Journal of Marketing*, 63(special issue), 168–79.

Stinchcomb, A. L. (1965), Social structure and organizations, in: March, J. G. (ed.), *Handbook of Organisations*, Rand McNally, Chicago, IL, pp. 142–93.

The Economist (2007), To avoid the Big-C, stay small, 3 November, 85–6.

Tripsas, M. (1997), Unraveling the process of creative destruction: complementary assets and incumbent survival in the typesetter industry, *Strategic Management Journal*, 18(Summer Special Issue), 119–42.

Webb, J. W., Ireland, R. D., Hitt, M. A., Kistruck, G. M. and Tihanyi, L. (2011), Where is the opportunity without the customer? An integration of marketing activities, the entrepreneurship process, and institutional theory, *Journal of the Academy of Marketing Science*, 39(4), 537–54.

Weitz, B. A., Sujan, H. and Sujan, M. (1986), Knowledge, motivation, and adaptive behavior: a framework for improving selling effectiveness, *Journal of Marketing*, 50(October), 174–91.

Westphal, J. D., Gulati, R. and Shortell, S. M. (1997), Customization or conformity? An institutional and network perspective on the content and consequences of TQM adoption, *Administrative Science Quarterly*, 42(June), 366–94.

Woodruff, R. B. (1997), Customer value: the next source for competitive advantage, *Journal of the Academy of Marketing Science*, 25(2), 139–53.

Workman, J. P., Jr. (1993), Marketing's limited role in new product development in one computer systems firm, *Journal of Marketing Research*, 30(4), 405–21.

Wouters, J. P. M. and Nijssen, E. J. (2012), *Understanding Adoption Behavior of Innovators*, Working Paper, Eindhoven University of Technology, Eindhoven, The Netherlands.

Zhao, M., Hoeffler, S. and Dah, D. W. (2012), Imagination difficulty and new product evaluation, *Journal of Product Innovation Management*, 29(S1), 76–90.

Index

validation of the business model 9;
  tests for 9
valley of death 150
value 4, 12, 35–6; exchange 4, 5;
  perceived value 36; of product 4;

proposition 39; to target segment 38;
  see also customer value
venturesome customers 26, 57;
  see also lead customers
viral marketing 122

Taylor & Francis eBooks

Helping you to choose the right eBooks for your Library

Add Routledge titles to your library's digital collection today. Taylor and Francis ebooks contains over 50,000 titles in the Humanities, Social Sciences, Behavioural Sciences, Built Environment and Law.

Choose from a range of subject packages or create your own!

Benefits for you
» Free MARC records
» COUNTER-compliant usage statistics
» Flexible purchase and pricing options
» All titles DRM-free.

Benefits for your user
» Off-site, anytime access via Athens or referring URL
» Print or copy pages or chapters
» Full content search
» Bookmark, highlight and annotate text
» Access to thousands of pages of quality research at the click of a button.

REQUEST YOUR
FREE
INSTITUTIONAL
TRIAL TODAY

Free Trials Available
We offer free trials to qualifying academic, corporate and government customers.

eCollections – Choose from over 30 subject eCollections, including:

Archaeology	Language Learning
Architecture	Law
Asian Studies	Literature
Business & Management	Media & Communication
Classical Studies	Middle East Studies
Construction	Music
Creative & Media Arts	Philosophy
Criminology & Criminal Justice	Planning
Economics	Politics
Education	Psychology & Mental Health
Energy	Religion
Engineering	Security
English Language & Linguistics	Social Work
Environment & Sustainability	Sociology
Geography	Sport
Health Studies	Theatre & Performance
History	Tourism, Hospitality & Events

For more information, pricing enquiries or to order a free trial, please contact your local sales team: www.tandfebooks.com/page/sales

Routledge
Taylor & Francis Group

The home of
Routledge books

www.tandfebooks.com